Growing Up
In The *Greatest*
Generation

FRANK CLYMER

ISBN 978-1-64079-839-7 (paperback)
ISBN 978-1-64079-840-3 (digital)

Christian Faith Publishing, Inc.
832 Park Avenue
Meadville, PA 16335
www.christianfaithpublishing.com

Printed in the United States of America

Dedication

I dedicate this book to my dear wife of fifty-nine years, Leila.

She was always an encouragement to me and especially as she knew I wanted to do this new adventure.

Her constant comment to me as I was writing was, "How can you remember so much and so many details about your youth so many years ago?" She would laugh that maybe she could write one or two pages of her own first twelve years. I know that wasn't true.

I don't think she ever knew the full impact her words would have on me throughout our entire marriage when she said, "Frank, I know you can do anything you put your mind to do."

I still don't believe it.

She was the Lord's gift to me.

We knew love.

Contents

Acknowledgments

To my three children Jim, Karen, Lois and their spouses, my grandchildren, my brothers and sister, nieces and nephews, and good friends who enjoyed the early writing of this true story and then encouraged me to get it published—thank you.

Introduction

Many of us have read accounts of the "greatest generation," but they were always written by adults as they either read or experienced it. What makes this story different and will keep your interest from other accounts is you will be seeing it from a childhood view as I actually lived through it and had so many experiences to draw from. Children see and experience things differently than adults. I believe there is an honesty and simplicity in their observation that is many times lost as we mature into adult life.

Fortunately, I was blessed with a good memory and was able to recall details to all I will write about. If you like nostalgia, I know you will enjoy this book. I will take you back to the good old days, and you will live it with me no matter what your age.

I will try to show you how life was lived during the greatest generation and how the war affected everything we did by using our family, neighborhood, and community to tell the story. The things we went through were typical for the time, and yet our community and neighborhood was unusual.

For instance, our small town of 2,500, which was made up mostly of German people called the Pennsylvania Germans or Pennsylvania Dutch, produced five generals, one in the First World War, three from the Second World War, and one after the war. We were a very patriotic community. Sellersville, with our good neighbor Perkasie, through the sale of war bond stamps through schoolchildren and adults purchased a B-17 bomber for the US Army Air Force and named it the *Spirit of Sell-Perk*.

Because of our heavy German population, the Nazi Party established a German American Bund Camp before the war at the edge of our community. I'll share the personal contact I had with a family on our street who had sons in this youth camp and our reaction from the community about this camp.

There was even a Warner Bros. movie called *The Pride of the Marines,* which showed our local hero's part who died at Guadalcanal in the Solomon Islands. He was an orphaned Native American boy named John Rivers, who was credited with killing over two hundred Japanese in one night. I will give you details of his life and this battle, which is quite interesting.

I had four uncles who also fought in the war. This made the war even more personal for us. The first two were US Army; one fought in Europe and enlisted as soon as war was declared and his brother, who dropped out of school to also join the army and fought in the Philippine islands. Of special note, I'll explain later in the story that I had two uncles who fought in the Russian Army against the Nazis, and both were killed.

I will be sharing with you the sacrifices made by Americans during the war and how our everyday activities were affected. We will talk about the ration stamps for gas, food, etc. The scrap drives, music, movies, news, air-raid drills, purchasing war bond stamps, the military drafts, loved ones lost and wounded—all the things that changed our lives forever.

Was it challenging? Yes. Would I exchange it for anything? No. It was the greatest generation. I will be covering happenings in my life and family background in order to show how things really were at this time that led us to become the greatest generation.

8 years old   *12 years old*
As I looked growing up in this time period.

10

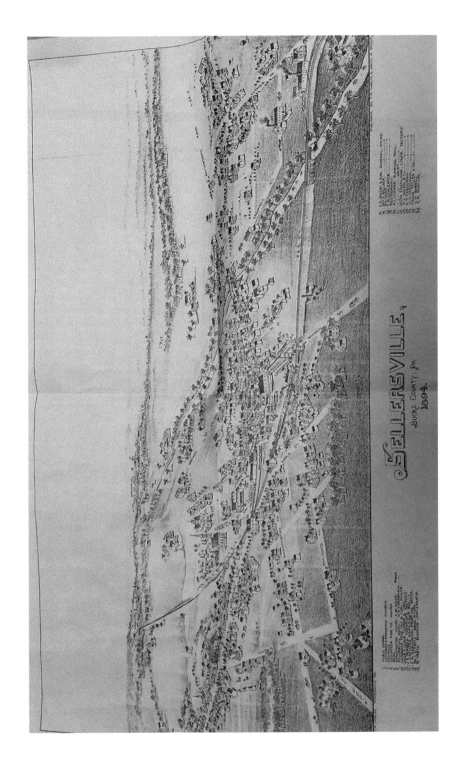

SELLERSVILLE,
BUCKS COUNTY, PA.
1894.

1

Sellersville

*Main St looking north opposite of Post office
and Washington House Hotel.*

Sellersville, Pa

North Main Street and Washington House Hotel. Walter Baum's house on left side with American flag.

The town this story takes place in is Sellersville, Pennsylvania, nestled in the rolling hills in rural beautiful Bucks County, approximately thirty-five miles northwest of Philadelphia. It was founded in 1738 and located on what is now known as the Liberty Trail because the Liberty Bell was moved from Philadelphia to Allentown, Pennsylvania, in order to hide it in a church building since the British were coming into Philadelphia.

There are still two buildings standing and in use today that have existed from the founding of the town, the Washington House hotel and the Old Mill building. Both are proud symbol of our heritage. Pictures of both are in the next chapter.

What makes this or any community different from other communities? It is citizenry. At the time of my youth, you really don't come to appreciate the people who are affecting your life, but as time passes and you reflect back, you have a new perspective.

The community was friendly but reserved. Men especially held back all emotions except when it came to joking and laughing. It was a happy community as was our home. Even though love was seldom shown outwardly within the home, there was an atmosphere of love, peace, and caring that is difficult to describe.

As Sellersville had a strong German heritage, this was also reflected in our speaking. Older adults would speak a dialect of German called Pennsylvania Dutch, i.e., German. This was a mixture of German and English but definitely German sounding.

When I was a boy, I enjoyed hearing adults speak it. I never learned it but for a dozen words. We had neighbors who spoke it and two ladies who lived on either side of us spoke to each other every time they saw each other. They would always be laughing as they spoke; maybe they were talking about me. This was a great advantage older people had over the younger generation. Today there is hardly anyone who speaks it.

If you travel fifty miles to Lancaster County where Amish people live, you will hear it all the time. A step back in time.

My father could speak it but not very fluently as he aged because his generation was dying off. But he loved to converse because for that generation, it was really fun, and as I said, they were always laughing.

I asked my father once, "Why is it always so funny?"

His reply was, "In Pennsylvania Dutch, it just comes out so different than English."

A note of interest, when he was a child, many homes only spoke German. In his home, they spoke English and Pennsylvania Dutch, so he had no trouble when starting school, but many of his first-grade classmates did have this problem.

Like most communities, Sellersville went through its own industrial evolution. From cigar making, 1880-1920 to men's trousers, 1920-1970 and the U.S. Gauge Company, 1910-1990. The German population always seemed to have a special aptitude to anything mechanical and so it was with the success of the Gauge Company and many machine shops that followed in and around our community.

SELLERSVILLE, PA. 1936-1948

GROCERY STORES

MY FATHERS' HOME

NOBLE ST.

CIGAR BOX FACTORY

ST. AGNES R.C. CHURCH

SELLERSVILLE CEMETERY

ST. MICHAELS LUTHERN CH.

LAWN AVE.

WASHINGTON AVE.

CHURCH ST.

ELEMENTRY SCHOOLS

READING R.R.

MY HOME AT 1949

GREEN ST.

R.R. STATION

BAUM HOME

ST PAULS REFORMED CH

ODD FELLOWS HALL

FREDERICKS' BARBER SHOP

TEMPLE AVE.

WASHINGTON HOUSE

TEMPLE AVE.

POST OFFICE

N. MAIN ST.

MAPLE AVE.

SELLERSVILLE PLAYGROUND

WALNUT ST.

TROLLEY STATION

LAKE LENAPE PARK

FIRE HOUSE

DAM

SCOUT CABIN

LAKE LENAPE

LAKE LENAPE

OLD MILL

STEELYS GAS STATION

PARK AVE.

PARK AVE.

CLYMER HOMESTEAD

S. MAIN ST.

DIAMOND ST.

PANTS FACTORY

HUGHES AVE.

MANNS STORE

CLYMER AVE.

CLYMER AVE.

U.S. GAUGE

2

A Walk Down Town

Since we are talking about the people of Sellersville, let's take a walk through the town and meet some of these people and go into the stores and shops as I did as a boy. I think you will find it interesting. We won't walk too fast, but it won't take long.

The dam at Lake Lenape, the beginning of our beautiful park system.

Autumn on the walk and bike trail at Lake Lenape.

The east branch of the Perkiomen Creek divides the town in half. We refer to it as Lake Lenape, named after the Lenape Indian tribe that lived in our area. The stream is about sixty feet wide and four feet to five feet deep with a five-foot-high dam that creates this depth. These dimensions hold true for about two miles. Because of the dam, there was made an outstanding, beautiful park system through Sellersville and our sister town of Perkasie to the east of us. It also features a beautiful bike and walking trails that extend for about three miles.

We will begin on the south side of town, which we also called Jersey. I'm guessing it was called this because it lay on the south side of Lake Lenape, just like New Jersey on the other side of the Delaware River.

We will stay on Main Street starting at Clymer Avenue. This street was named after our great-grandparents' large homestead located on the western side of the railroad tracks and also two of Dad's uncles, who had a woodworking and gristmill just off Clymer Avenue along the railroad tracks.

Mann's Grocery Store, southwest corner of Clymer Ave. and Main Street.

Typical grocery store you encountered while doing your grocery shopping. This photo shows the American Store at Main and Maple avenue. (Courtesy of Sellersville Museum)

At Main and Clymer Avenues was a grocery store owned by Franklin Mann. This was a typical grocery store that Dad shopped at for several years. This was one of eight grocery stores located in town. You must remember everyone shopped local. Many ladies walked to the store with a wicker basket on their arm and made several small purchases a week, or their husbands drove and parked the car at the curb near the store.

Once in the store, you walked up to the counter and either handed the clerk your list of groceries or read them off to him, and they would quickly find the groceries and bring them back to the counter. There was not a large selection, but no one ever lacked anything. The wives, I guess, had to do more real home cooking.

These stores were always warm and friendly because they could not afford to lose you as a customer. There was always conversation between you and the clerks or owners.

Mann's Grocery Store was the first to introduce frozen food and grocery carts. This was really big stuff for a small town. They even had an opening night with food and drink treats and small give-aways. I was there that night with some of my friends from Hughes Avenue. The featured frozen food company was Birds Eye frozen vegetables and fruits.

Mann's Store was located looking north, on the lower left corner of the intersection of Clymer Avenue and Main Street. The large US Gauge plant was located on the right side of Main Street and fronted Clymer Avenue.

Coming back to the left side again, there was a Hoffman Dairy Ice Cream Stand that was open in the summer, directly across the street from Mann's Store. This was a small wooden structure with a wooden ground-level deck where you could sit and eat your treats. They were not spraying mosquitoes yet, so good luck!

The monument at Diamond and South Main Street.

Let's journey down to Main Street and Park Avenue. This was always our busy intersection, and we got our first red light soon after the Second World War. On the right side at Main and Diamond Streets was the First World War Soldiers' Memorial, which now stands at the new memorial area in Lake Lenape.

People standing in front of Wm. Steeleys' gas station at intersection of Main, Diamond and Park avenue observing the flooding.
(Courtesy of Sellersville Museum)

Bill Steeley's Pennico Gas Station was also on the right side of Park and Main. Nace's State Farm Insurance is now there. Steeley's Gas Station was important while I was growing up. The owner, Bill Steeley, was a good man with an interest in the well-being of the community and was known by everyone. I bought my silver King Schwinn bike from him with my newspaper money for, I believe, seventy-nine dollars. Dad also bought a bike for Mother, but she never used it.

His gas station was the closest store where you could buy popsicles or Dixie Cup ice cream, candy bars and sodas, so it was a popular place. If I ever write the rest of my life story, there is much more to reminisce about as a teenager

Wm. "Bill" Steeley was a likable and respected businessman. Ardent promoter and supporter of amature hard ball baseball teams in the community. (Courtesy of Sellersville Museum)

Yes, that's me with my Schwinn Silver King bike. Using it every day that I bought 70 years ago.

and working on our cars and just hanging out at night.

On the other side of Park Avenue from Steeley's was another gas station that sold Atlantic Refinery products. Then next to his station was the Old Mill Building, which was closed during the war, but I'm not sure why. It could be he was serving in the military. After the war, Willard Buck opened Buck's Furniture Store, which sold a top grade of furniture and was there for fifty years. Leila and I bought our girls' bedroom suite and kitchen set with counter stools that are in use today by the family.

The old Mill Building on South Main Street. The oldest building in Sellersville. 1740

Directly across the street was Fred Schaffner's car repair garage, which was located in what was once a barn. He later moved to South Main Street where the Sellersville Drugstore is now located. Next to Schaffner's was a small Esso gasoline station. National Penn Bank occupies this area now.

Let's keep heading north over the bridge past the Sellersville Fire Company, on the left, that was so important and a proud part of our community. So many of our citizens served so proudly there. Across Main Street from the firehouse was the all-important Lehigh Valley Trolley Station that so many people relied upon to get them to local towns, and as far as Philadelphia and Allentown. We used it to go to the Plaza Movie Theater in Perkasie for those cowboy double features on Monday and Tuesday nights. I can still feel the movement and swaying of the car and sound on the tracks.

Sellersville Firehouse with turn of the century fire alarm ring.

On the same side of the street as the trolley station was Fritz Schleuben's Drugstore. This is where, as kids, we would stop on our way to school and buy our penny candy. Our little brown bags were often filled with choices that we changed our minds several times each. Fritz would stand back behind the candy, which had a glass front about five feet high and forty inches wide with a half-dozen shelves, and say in a German accent, "Now make up your mind."

Fritz's also sold ice cream, and when the floods would come, the store would be flooded, and they would have to give it away because they were very close to Lake Lenape that the Perkiomen Creek flowed through. I bought my mother's first Christmas present here, a small bottle of Evening in Paris perfume. We also purchased Valentine's cards, Halloween faces, and other items that fascinated us as kids and were part of our young lives. Here again it was the personalities of Mr. and Mrs. Schleuben who were so kind and understanding to us as children that made the community what it was.

Continuing a few more buildings, we come to the Moose Hall, now the American Legion. This is where Mike Hallman's Christmas party was held because of its large auditorium. I remember being inside with my dad only a few times. There was a bar there, and you could buy light meals like hamburgers, sandwiches, etc. They also had gambling slot machines inside. I guess they were legal, but they were there, and Dad pointed out the cook at that time lost his whole pay in one day playing it. He should have known you can't beat the system.

Now we are coming into the heart of town with so many stores, very little parking, and Route 309 coming right through the town. The community was so proud to have the state run this highway through town thinking this would create a goldmine for the town. It never worked. People just drove through the town, and we were left with a busy stream of traffic and the problems it brings.

Pennsylvania Power and Light had their local offices and maintenance trucks in a building just before the corner of Main and Walnut Streets. You could pay your electric bills there.

Main Street looking north. Main business district.

On the corner of Main and Walnut Streets on the south side was Smith's Grocery Store. This store had a large tin roof in the front that extended to the whole sidewalk. It reminded you of the Old West stores. I was only in this store a few times, and, because of the extended roof, it always seemed dark inside, even with all the lights on. Fluorescent lights were not invented yet. This building was torn down after the war, and the current apartment buildings were built. They had great clearance sales before the demolition began, and my friends and I were there looking for buys. We ended up all buying strawhats, the old-fashioned ones with flat tops for ten cents each, quite a buy, and we had a great time showing them off.

Cross over Walnut Street and you will find another grocery store, Hildelbatle's Store, which closed around 1947 or 1948, because Earl Moyer's Electric Appliance Store, where I first saw a working television set showing a Phillies game on a Saturday afternoon, took over. Another item of interest was when Ken Huff and I got a temporary job there delivering Christmas circulars to homes in town and Souderton and Telford.

Hildelbatle's grocery store which later became Moyer's Electric appliance store at N.E. corner of Main and Walnut streets. Store is at center of photo. Apartment building at right replaced Smith's store after the war.

Some of the money I earned I spent back in the store to buy my mother the large metallic and china fruit dish that she kept in her kitchen the rest of her life and now resides with my daughter Karen Hausman, and it still looks good.

Let's cross Main Street, back at Main and Walnut, to the left side and go up the busy corridor, at least for us. Yep, another grocery store, the A&P Store at the first corner of the building. If we ran out of bread, milk, etc., Mother would send me there. People loved their coffee, as well as, I am sure, many other groceries. Every time I was sent for sliced white bread, I would love to smell the aroma and then take the loaf and squeeze it together like an accordion to see how small I could make it. You would be surprised, try it some time. I always made sure it was stretched back to normal size, but I'm not sure it was quite the right size.

Same side of the street in the same row of buildings was the Sellersville Savings and Loan where I got my first house mortgage, and next to it, for a short time, was a very small five-and-dime store. Then it was Earl Moyer's Electric Appliance Store before he moved across the street to the Hildelbatle building.

Then a new set of buildings where the American Legion had occupied. They were very important in the community because of the patriotic influence, the parades they led and treating participants after the parades, being involved in everything positive for our country, and, most of all, a place our returning war veterans could identify. They awarded me first place in the Memorial Day poster contest, just another example of the many things they and the ladies' auxiliary were involved in.

Next to them was the Sellersville Hardware Store where a Mr. Kline and Mr. Fretz were the owners. You could buy all your hardware needs there, and they also carried a nice assortment of metal cap pistols after the war that kept me coming into the store to check them out.

The Sellersville Restaurant took up two building spaces. It was owned by the Weiss family. They featured a soda and ice cream bar on one side and the restaurant on the other, although there was no permanent separation of the two. It was really the only restaurant in town where you could get a regular meal besides the Washington

House. Uncle Joe would take us here to buy banana splits for Anna, Paul, and myself every time he came to visit during and after the war.

At the very corner of the block of buildings was the Acme store. They also rented a double space. They featured meats since they had a separate butcher shop in the store, and a family friend, Albert Lawrence, ran that department. Later, he had his own store in town and featured the butcher shop. At one time, he lived next door to us on Hughes Avenue, and it was his garage that another friend of mine and myself threw paint all over the inside of the garage.

The Acme store closed some time after the war and Earl Cressman and Russel Raudenbush opened Earl Russel Men's Clothing Store for some years. It seemed very popular since both men were well-known.

Cross over Maple Avenue and you have the post office that really hasn't changed its appearance through the years. I would love to go with Arto Crouthamel when he had business to do there. I would stand inside and gaze and study the beautiful wall mural, painted during the Depression of the 1930s in order to keep artists painting during this difficult time. I still enjoy it today and show a photo of it. It is a picture of the various ways mail was delivered at that time, showing the planes, trains, ships, and trucks of that era. The smell of paper and ink still lingers today.

Sellersville Post Office that has not changed since my childhood.

Wall mural inside post office.

Washington House Hotel

The landmark Washington House was very popular to townsfolk then and even more so today with the theater. It was the only place you could rent a room without going into someone's house. I would use their toilets when needed before or after serving newspapers since Jake Esser's newsstand and our assembly station were directly across the street in the corner basement.

Walter Crouthamel's Grocery Store was across from the hotel on the left side of Main Street and Temple Avenue. Walter also had a successful store. He was a small man in stature, but very friendly and talkative, living on Diamond Street. It was in this same apartment building that I rented an apartment on the third floor in the rear of the building. When Leila and I lived there, Francis Roeder bought the business from Walter and continued a successful business.

Applebach's Antique Store was next to our apartment building, which was home to Virginia Applebach, our high school art teacher. She served well in our community, especially with historical information.

Let's step back to the right of Main Street on the south side of Temple Avenue and Main Street to see the large white building with the second-floor bay window. This was the home of artist and writer Walter Baum when he was a boy. In the basement was Jake Esser's newsstand where we met to travel up to the train station for our newspapers in Jake's old Model T Ford.

Above us was a small five-and-dime store where I would always go to buy my glass marbles to play our marble games in the dirt. We often would play that any marbles you knocked out of the ring, you could keep. I just figured out why I was always back buying marbles.

Artist Walter Baum's home where he was raised.
Basement entrance years later was Jake Esser's newspaper store
where I began serving the evening bulletin Philadelphia paper.

*Main Street looking South from Washinton House and
Walter Baum's home as a boy on left.*

*Odd Fellows Building or I.O.O.F.
Temple at the northeast corner of
Main Street and Temple Avenue.*

On the end side of Main and Temple was Walter Baum's father's barbershop that closed probably before the war ended. After the war, a ladies' shop opened and occupied the whole upper floor. Note of interest: Dad's cousin, Byron Sheetz, owned this building. It could have been in the '60s to '80s.

Directly across from the building on Main and Temple was the Odd Fellows Building. This is a four-story building. On the third floor was where my brother Paul and I would play bingo on Saturday evenings. It was an old building even then with dry wooden floors that creaked sometimes as you walked on them.

The first floor on the corner was Krebs Drugstore. This store was later owned by the Allen family. When Krebs owned it, we could buy a milkshake for fifteen cents, but no ice cream was included. It cost twenty cents with ice cream.

Frederick's Barbershop was actually another landmark because of the personalities that gathered there. It was owned by two brothers Charlie and Lloyd Frederick. I got many haircuts here and would love to sit and listen to the conversations, especially by the regular, everyday shave customers, who either knew or thought they knew many of the solutions to local and international politics and sports—it was a grand time.

Walk back to Main Street and north to Sellersville National Bank, the local hometown bank. Then the second house from the bank was Lee Wilhelam's Funeral Home. Lee was a good citizen in the town. He served the community in an unbelievable position. He was a fireman who fielded every fire call that came in for the company, and he sounded the fire sirens. If you had a fire, your call went to this home, and most people never knew it. He never took a vacation; either he, his wife, or adult daughter were always there. Incredible! Arthur Crouthamel was buried from this home, and I visited families and paid respects numerous times here.

Lee Wilhelam's Funeral Home on North Main Street,
to the left is Walter Baum's home.

Probably the best-known personality ever to live in the Sellersville area was Walter E. Baum, the famous artist who lived at Main and Green Streets. He painted and also sold his artwork

Walter Emerson Baum

there. He was a very gifted man. He was an art critic for the evening *Philadelphia Bulletin* in Philadelphia, writer for the *Poultry Item* magazine, wrote a history on Sellersville, and probably many other publications. He established the Baum School of Art in Allentown and the Allentown Art Museum. He was well respected in the field of art throughout the United States and other countries.

Like most artists, they really become famous when

they die, and their picture prices soar through the roof because there are no more. This happened to all his artwork. They are now very, very expensive. We children could earn a nickel from him by posing holding a broom, shovel, etc., as he would quickly sketch a stick figure of you. He would take us through his studio from time to time, showing us what he was currently working on. I always found it interesting to see things in the making.

If you continue up Main Street Hill, the Triangle Lumber Company was on the right and a feed mill for animals on the left where I would by rabbit pellets for a rabbit we had on Hughes Avenue.

Just before the Main Street train bridge was the railroad foot bridge that was taken down sometime ago but was very important to people and children coming to the elementary schools on Church Street and pedestrians crossing into the shopping areas. Chief Mike Hallman was usually at the bridge helping the children to cross.

I remember as a small child, maybe five or six years old, seeing a coal truck turned over lying on its side on the embankment next to the old Main Street that goes down to the railroad tracks.

There were two more grocery stores in Sellersville when I was a child; they were at Maple and Lawn Avenues, owned by Ralph Heckler and, before him, Os Nase and, later, Curt Meinhold.

On Washington Avenue, there was a small store owned by Irwin Fretz, who also worked with Dad in North Wales and then for him when Dad was involved with his own businesses. The store was still in operation when I lived on Washington Avenue in the 1960s, but under different ownership.

Oil painting by Walter E. Baum of North Main Street
as it still looks today, but minus the sled.

One valuable thing that these stores supplied to the community were the personalities who owned and worked the stores. They supplied a positive influence in all our lives. The Pennsylvania blue laws were in effect, so no stores were open on Sunday. It is interesting how we ever got by with no shopping at all on Sunday.

There were only three larger factories in town, and most people in town would walk to them. The US Gauge plant on Clymer Avenue employed two thousand people. Lutz's pants factory at Park Avenue and Hughes Avenue employed about one hundred people. The Penn Pants Co. at Maple and Lawn Avenue also employed about one hundred people. This was run by a respected man named Walter Soltau.

U.S. Gauge Co. located on Clymer Ave.

Three churches served the community: Saint Agnes Roman Catholic Church was just a small edifice, which still stands on North Main Street; St. Michael's Lutheran Church at Main and Church

Streets, where our family attended; and St. Paul's Reformed Church at Green and Penn Streets.

I hope this walk gave you a picture of my Sellersville during 1936-1948. I thought you might enjoy it because no one will ever experience it again.

3

Family

Mom and dad at Lake Lenape across from Sea Scout Cabin, 1942.

I would like to share briefly who I am, my siblings, parents, and grandparents. I think you will find this interesting because in all families there is a rich story of struggles, defeats, and achievements. You will see how both sides of our family, beginning with paternal and maternal grandparents, faced unbelievable obstacles but persevered and overcame them chasing the American dream.

We will be referring in the following pages stories of my parents, but let me say at this point, how blessed we were to have these parents that the Lord gave us. They were always in charge, we were the children, they were the parents. The roles were never reversed, although sometimes in our teenage years we thought we might reverse it. It did not work.

My mother Anna Luduinowich Duch Clymer.

No parents, I mean no parents gave and sacrificed more for their family than they did. We, their children, were central. We were never spoiled. We were directed and disciplined as needed. I can honestly say we loved our parents and never wanted to disappoint them. They showed their love mostly by their actions to us. It was not huggy kissy, but words and protection from harm and fear.

Even though Dad worked long and hard, it seemed he was always there for us. Mother worked in the men's pants sewing factories most of the time as we were growing up, yet it seemed she was always there for us. She worked at Lutz's pants factory building at the bottom of Hughes Avenue, which I and my brother Barry purchased for our company in our adult years. Children sitters were always provided for us, and they were very good young ladies obeying our mother's directions.

Our parents showed us in their words and lives how we were to live and act toward one another and the world we were in.

My father Franklin S. Clymer.

Lutz's Pants Factory where mother worked. Brother Barry
and myself purchased it years later for our own company.

4

My Father's Family

I am going to begin with my paternal grandmother, Anna Catherine Scheetz Clymer, 1872-1943. I do not have a lot of memories, but I do remember very clearly the following, along with stories my father would tell me about his mother.

She became a widow in 1917, when she lost her husband to double pneumonia while working at Bethlehem Steel during the First World War. Dad never talked much about his father because he was only eight years old when he died, but he did mention that he worked for the Reading Railroad, and I believe it was doing rail maintenance.

Dad Clymer's parents wedding picture.
Anna Scheetz Clymer and Wilson Beischer Clymer

When the war started, he went to work at Bethlehem Steel in Bethlehem, Pennsylvania. He would take the train every day to work, but when, on the return trip home, the men often were wet with sweat or water from showering and hurrying to make the train, he came down with pneumonia in both lungs. Dad's cousin, Harold Clymer, Jim Clymer and Janice Rush's father, was in the bedroom the day before he died and told me what he heard and saw as a boy.

Pastor Weidliech of St. Michael's Lutheran Church was called in that day. He was also a family friend and told Dad's father, Wilson, that he was going to die very soon, and there was no hope, and he would prepare himself for this happening. Wilson replied he did not think that would happen and believed he could get better. I know no more about his spiritual life, but he came from a Mennonite family. Rockhill Mennonite Church near Sellersville and Telford is where the family of Wilson's parents and many relatives attended.

Bicylce Club: Wilson 2nd row second from right.

As a young man, Wilson belonged to a bicycle club, and a photograph showing him with his friends in the club is in the family possessions. These clubs were very popular at about the turn of the century, and, not being biased, he is the best-looking man on the photo.

Dad's brother Wilson who died at 14 years of age in the accident at the Sellersville quarry.

There were five children born to the family. The oldest child died about four years of age to diphtheria. His name was Paul. My father being the youngest! To compound the loss of her husband, her fourteen-year-old son, Wilson, was killed at the Sellersville Quarry near North Main Street, Sellersville, across from Faith Baptist Church.

A group of boys, about five or six, were playing on the weekend in the quarry, and Wilson was at the top when the whole ledge left loose and fell about fifty feet and crushed his leg. Because of the severe loss of

blood (remember there were no transfusions at this time 1919), a day or two later he died.

My grandmother must have been a very determined person and a hard worker. She was determined to keep the family together and successfully raised them.

My father seemed to have a normal childhood with the stories he told me and a happy childhood with his friends and many activities, especially working as a young boy. He understood

Franklin S. Clymer as a boy about the time he lost his father.

43

from his mother he would also have to do his part to earn money, I suppose to help take care of his own needs. He had many chores around the house and helping his mother with delivery of washed and ironed clothing in his express wagon, which he took to relatives and neighbors all over Sellersville. He would usually get a tip from these people, and this he could keep.

His mother, my grandmother, supported the family by taking in washing and ironing, along with housecleaning. His sister, Martha, had a job as a teenager in a factory in Perkasie that make fine yarn and thread. I am sure she gave almost all her earnings to her mother, besides helping with the ironing every night.

His older brother, Irwin, also just began working, and he also gave his money home. Because of the loss of their father, the finances were such that all the children left school after the eighth grade. Irwin had told me that he had always done well in school, and his Lutheran pastor, who my grandmother also cleaned for, said he would help support him if he would go to college. But he chose not to and learned the electrician trade where he was one of the most respected in that field in our area.

My father lost his father when he was eight years old. Besides his laundry job, he found many other avenues of work. Besides doing lawn work in summer, he worked at Jackson's Greenhouse shoveling dirt and making flowerbeds in the greenhouse, which was hot and hard work. He cleaned tobacco spittoons in factories within the borough, most of them where they rolled and made cigars, which was the major employer within the community. This job was to take these metal pots with their own special shapes and dump the contents that men had chewed and spit their tobacco into all day long. After washing each pot clean, I can only imagine the germs he was exposed to.

He also worked at the Sellersville Hotel, which was torn down before I was born. This was located on Main Street, across from the small park in downtown. I know one of his jobs was to take hot dogs with sauerkraut to Lake Lenape where the War Memorial stands and sell them to the Sellersville football fans that gathered for the football games. He would call out to the fans, "A loaf of bread and a pound of meat and all the mustard you can eat, Hot Dogs!"

When he was in the eighth grade, he also left school and began working at the Sellers Cigar Box Company, being located directly across the street from his home on Noble Street.

Sellers Cigar Box factory, Noble Street, near Main.

He told the story before he could legally work at the box company, they left him work there but was told if any state officials came through, he was to leave immediately and go home. One day this happened when a child labor law official came through, and my father barely escaped. But he left his winter coat hanging where he was working. I don't think the company got in trouble, and he continued to work there but made sure his jacket was never left behind again.

The box factory was still operating when I was a boy because we would go there and ask for the scrap wood. These were long, narrow pieces that we cut to the correct lengths and make our homemade flying kites using newspaper and string with glue. Monroe Sellers was still living; he owned the factory and lived into his nineties. He was also a descendent of the family Sellersville derived its name from. He

Monroe Sellers shown in a earlier photo. Sellersville derived its name from his family line that owned the Sellers Tavern. (Courtesy of Sellersville Museum)

was a tall, thin man with white hair and looked like a Charles Dickens character.

I relate these stories to my grandmother because she was the person loved and respected, and she successfully guided the family through this challenging period of life. I do remember her, even at my young age. She never appeared as a strong lady, but gentle and smiling, with a slight Pennsylvania Dutch accent. I remember sleeping over at her home on Noble Street with my Aunt Martha and Uncle Frank living with her, and me going with Uncle Frank into Perkasie on a Saturday morning to do some shopping at Seventh and Market Streets.

She was a very good cook and seamstress. Because I was such a big boy as a young child, when my parents would buy me clothes and when it came to suits, they had to buy older boys' or young men's clothing, and she would adjust them to fit me. She did a lot of crocheting, and some of her work is still in family hands.

Dad and Mother both told the story when Mother ate at Grandmother's for the first time and was never told they were having fried and breaded cow's brains. Mother said they were very good, but never had them again!

Around 1942, it was decided to sell the home on Noble Street and build a one-story house at Diamond Street and Grandview Avenue, Sellersville. This was done because of our grandmother's failing health. I believe her health problems centered on the heart with hypertension and hardening of the arteries. I can still picture the steam shovel equipment to dig out the basement and going to view the progress several evenings every week. Uncle Irvin, of course, did the wiring.

Spring Wild fowers along Lake Lenope.

Diamond Street was paved onto their corner at Grandview Avenue. From their house to 113 at Silverdale was only a dirt road. Even building the new home to help her would not save her life.

I remember this next story often, especially in spring, about the month of May, when the wildflower, which I call pink-and-white flax. It still grows in many meadows. I picked a large bouquet in the field and told my mother I would like to walk these to Grammy Clymer, as we were then living on Hughes Avenue. She said I could, and I was on my way. I was seven years old at the time, and when I arrived, my Aunt Martha greeted me, telling me Grammy was sick and asleep in bed! I went into her bedroom and watched her silently for a few minutes, and Aunt Martha assured me she would vase the flowers for her. As simple as this story is, it is one I have and always will treasure.

Before I talk about the funeral, I need to say what my dad told me many years later. His mother would listen to gospel radio programs and especially a certain Bible preacher that I do not remember his name, but has given me some assurance of her salvation.

As far as I know, she was raised and died in the Lutheran church. I do believe in those days the church was more evangelistic. My grandmother's funeral is still very clear to me. This is the first time I ever experienced a person dying and attending a funeral.

The day of the funeral was a warm September afternoon. The funeral home was on Walnut Street in Sellersville that was owned by a relative, probably on the Scheetz side, and I have no remembrance of his name. It still has the glass-enclosed front sun porch and is located on the park side of the street.

The viewing was held at this house for about an hour. As we were leaving to travel to St. Michael's Lutheran Church, I remember my father standing just outside the front door and seeing him cry for the first time ever in my life. You must remember in those days men seldom showed their emotions.

At the church there was a small family service in a Sunday school room, the first room on the right as you entered the church. At the conclusion of the service, my Aunt Martha was given a white handkerchief, which she covered Grammy's face with. We proceeded to the family burial plot and committed her to the ground. The one request I remember she asked for concerning her death was she told the family she would like a cement outside box, which the family did, and I believe every member since has followed suit.

5

My Mother's Family

I want to share some history of Mother's side of the family. I found it to be a beautiful love story mixed with tragedy. Remember the movie *Doctor Zhivago*? Well, it's not exactly that story, but I'm sure there was snow.

My maternal grandfather Walter Ludwinowich

Grammy Duch, Edwina Wasilifa, was born in Russia on a farm outside of St. Petersburg. Her husband, our grandfather, Walter Ludwinowich, was a Polish soldier on a troop train traveling into Russia for friendly military maneuvers. The train stopped for water at her farm. She was at the water pump where they met. It was love at first sight. They exchanged addresses, and we are all here because of it.

They had two boys, Peter and Alexander, who they left with Grammy's parents, as they came to Philadelphia to settle before sending for the boys. But the Bolshevik revolution happened, and the boys were not allowed to leave. Grammy had contact with them until the

Second World War. They were in the Russian army and probably killed. Because neither they nor Grammy could ever make contact again.

Our mother and her sister Aunt Sophia were born in South Philadelphia. Mother was born September 17, 1914.

Our grandfather worked at Atlantic Refinery and was killed there in a terrible explosion. We do have his handsome military photograph in his white uniform with sword at his side.

Grammy married our grandfather's friend from Atlantic Refinery, who was also Polish and named Walter Duch. They had four children: Joseph, Rose, Walter, and Helen. This was not a good marriage because of his drinking. He

Maternal grandmother Edwino Wasilifo Ludwinowich

was also nice looking; he looked very much like President Dwight Eisenhower.

We would get to see them about four times a year. The most exciting visit would always be at Christmastime when we would leave for our one-day trip in Dad's 1937 to 1939 Plymouth or Dodge car, until after the war when he had a 1947 Ford Wagon and then the 1950 Plymouth wagon.

Mother would have our presents for Grammy, Aunt Helen, Uncle Walter, Uncle Joe and wife, Kate. Aunt Rose was only there during the war years, because she was living with us afterward and then was married in 1948. There were presents for Aunt Sophie and her children, which were so much appreciated by them because of the financial difficulties and poor living conditions. Aunt Sophie lived about fifteen minutes away, and we would usually spend about an hour with them. The presents we gave them were the only presents they would ever get, so they would be so excited to see us.

Grammy lived in a typical South Philadelphia row home in a Polish-Slavic area. There were no trees or grass, only brick and

Mother's brother Joe and sister Helen on South Phila front steps.

cement. The front of the houses had no porches, only stone steps down to the pavement and a narrow street. My mother told me when she was a child the streets were lit by gas lights by a man, the lamp lighter. Behind the house was a small yard about ten feet by fifteen feet with six-foot-high solid wooden fences, and about thirty yards from the back of the house was an elevated railroad.

It was always an exciting time to visit because South Philadelphia was so different from Sellersville's small-town surroundings. It was a long

Left to right: mother's brothers, Uncle Walter and Uncle Joe with Grammy Duch in her small back yard of cement and high wood fence in South Phily.

51

trip in those days, but the sights were interesting. I'm still writing about Christmas because as we traveled through Fairmont Park, one of the interesting things we saw were the park guards, i.e., park policeman standing in front of their little guard stands with probably hundred bottles of liquor in boxes and ribbons standing in front of each house with the guard standing with the bottles. This was a way the people showed their gratitude to them. Later this was abandoned.

There was excitement in the air. Usually no snow, but the same format was followed. Grammy Duch was always happy to see us as were all our aunts and uncles. There was always a tall, narrow tree in the living room. She would always make fried fish, mashed potatoes, vegetable, good bread, and her nut-filled rolled bread sometime in the afternoon.

Aunt Helen was someone we always loved, and we related to so well because she was only in her twenties and more like a tomboy in personality. She always had us on the go whenever we were with her. She would always take us to the corner bakery, where they made the largest cream and jelly donuts that were loaded. There was nothing like this back home. We would eat this sometimes before supper.

Christmas music would be played on a 45 rpm machine. Mario Lanza, the great singer from Philadelphia, was always featured at Christmas and brings back such great memories.

The one thing I dreaded about any of these trips was I would get motion sickness from the car ride. The first thing I had to do was go up the stairs and lay down for an hour or throw up and get it over with; then I was fine. This happened coming and leaving for home—I had the same problem.

6

The Children

I am the oldest of seven children, six boys and one sister. I was born in Sellersville's Grand View Hospital on March 9, 1936. Fortunately, and by the grace of God, we all turned out to be good citizens, involved in politics, successful in our occupations, and, most of all, firm believers in Jesus Christ as our Lord and Savior and involved in His work.

I'm retired in Florida after owning a safety protection clothing company with my brother Barry, who continues with the company. Paul had a long and very successful career for thirty-four years as a state representative in Harrisburg, Pennsylvania, where he chaired many important committees. Our sister, Anna, was a registered nurse where she spent most of her years in supervisory positions. Sad to say she is now deceased.

Brother Robert and youngest brother Jerry are retired public school teachers who impacted young peoples' lives with more than academics. Robert was also a winning coach in football, wrestling, and track. Brother David is a certified public accountant who has a very successful practice. I proudly—no, humbly—can say all were outstanding athletes in high school and college.

Left to right: (Back row) Paul, Franklin, Anna
(Front Row) Robert, David, 1943

7

Hughes Avenue

Vintage Early 40s

With the Stover home and the open fields east of Hughes Avenue as a background, some of the neighborhood children gather for a street photo: From left are: Dennis Huff, David Clymer, Nancy Minninger, Eddie Shelly, Paul Clymer (in back), Robert Clymer (Bubblegum), "Batsy" Minninger (in back), Peppie Minninger (wagon) Franklin Clymer (back), Dianne Minninger (front wagon), Bill Shelly (back wagon), Jimmy Shelly, in back, Richard Mitman, Kenny Huff, in back, Sharon Huff, Gary Huff and David Mullin. Most are parents and some are grandparents today. Paul Clymer is the 145th Assemblyman.

Classic photo of us children on Hughes Ave
with Mrs. Stover house behind us.

Within our borough was a street called Hughes Avenue. This is where I was raised from 1937-1948. My childhood is centered on these twenty row homes, ten on

55

Winter on Hughes Avenue. North end of dead end street with the open fields, Ziggy Shelly's plumber garage in background. I'm seated with Huff's dog named Beauty. Top left to right: Allen Crouthamel, brother Paul, Robert seated with Elain Mullen, Tommy Crouthamel and Ken Huff.

Winter on Hughes Ave. Myself throwing a lump of snow.

each side, that was dead-ended, so you only had neighborhood traffic. This street, at the time, seemed very normal but local history now tells us it wasn't. I say this because forty years later, the local newspaper is writing articles about this street, the exact years we spent our childhood there. All the things I will be telling you about, the neighbors (even gives our parents' names), the friendships, care for each other, games played, the impact we had on all our community, etc., was mentioned. In the article, Hughes Avenue, at the time, was called warm, secure, and even boastful. I believe the atmosphere that existed will never be captured and duplicated again.

We moved to 122 Hughes Avenue in Sellersville about 1937 or '38 because Paul did not live on Green Street where I lived as a baby. Our parents rented a third-floor apartment with no kitchen and no bath. They had to share this bathroom with the lady they rented from named Mrs. Smith who was a widow. They always made friends easily, and the friends they made there in a short time remained so for a lifetime.

Besides Mrs. Smith, there was Annie Benner and Arthur Crouthamel who moved in with us on Hughes Avenue. He had the back bedroom, our parents the front, and us children in the small middle room.

Hughes Avenue seems to absorb almost all my childhood because we lived there until 1948 when we moved to Green Street, near the top of the hill at number 27.

There were thirty-eight children living in these homes. I know there is always the tendency to look through the rose-colored glasses, and that's okay. The children actually did get along very well. Our activities were centered on playing, and that we did. In the summer it was baseball; autumn, football; sledding and playing in the snow for winter. All of our activities took place mainly on the street itself or down at the Lake Lenape Park and creek or up in the fields that led to Ketterer's Farm. Later the US Gauge bought and built there.

This time period was, of course, before television and air-conditioning, but not before radio. We would be out playing, but when four thirty to five thirty came about, we all headed to our homes to

My good buddy Paul growing up.

listen to *Jack Armstrong, the All-American Boy*; Tom Mix, the great cowboy; *Superman*; and we all know *Captain Midnight*, and others. They were only fifteen-minute shows, but how we hung on to every word, and how we saw the action in our minds.

Another exciting aspect of these shows was the commercials. They sold Ovaltine, Kellogg's Corn Pop cereal, Wheaties, Breakfast of Champions, etc. Then the most exciting part were the things we could send for that usually cost twenty-five cents to fifty cents, but we had to have them, no matter what. Some of the things offered were the secret decoder ring, the atomic ring that glowed in the dark, a secret whistle ring, and many other treasures. I remember there was something offered, and I begged Mother to send for it, which she eventually did and probably cost a quarter.

I would babysit my brother David after school by placing him in a child's stroller and place him on the pavement at Hughes Avenue while I played games in the street with my friends. Every so often I would push him up and down the sidewalk to keep him happy. Fortunately, he was a good and contented child. Seems like nothing has changed; he is still that person.

Left to Right: Franklin, Ann, and Paul. Notice the one year size difference between Paul and myself.

Anyway, I got twenty-five cents a week for this sitting. So, I made a deal if Mother would order this ring, I would do it free till it came. Well, two months later, it came. That's what I call a deal; thanks, Mom!

This was a family street, and the parents treated it this way. Many of the families did not even own a car, and those that did always parked them in their garages in the alleys. This kept our streets open for our macadam playground.

The automobiles that families owned, of course, were all from the pre-war days, the 1930's decade, since cars were not manufactured during the war. My father always drove Chrysler products like 1936 Plymouth and 1938 Dodge. He would change and repair his flat tires by patching the inner tubes in our garage as did most men. There were a few older cars that had to be started some times by turning a crank located between the front bumper and the radiator. There were some families that did not own a car. Remember, you worked in town like the U.S. Gauge, shopped in town, went to church in town, doctors, etc., so you could easily walk to everything. If other transportation was needed, you could use the trolley, train or the town taxi.

As kids we were like kids today with interest in cars by admiring and dreaming of the day we would drive one ourselves. There was a treat parents could give the children with these cars. In the summer we could jump on the running boards located at the bottom of the doors used to step on to get into the cars. They were exposed permanently as part of the structure.

Since no cars were air conditioned, the windows were always down in the summer. We would step on and hold on where the windows were down and get a great ride up our alley, all with our father's permission. In the summer he would always take his car to Lake Lenape to wash it with a bucket, sponge and shammy cloth to dry it clean. He always took pride in his cars and always kept them in repair and clean.

It seemed like it snowed more when I was a child and it seemed to last longer, which reminds me that every car was equipped with metal chains that were always used in heavy snow. The men would strap these chains over the two rear tires for traction in the snow. When the snow melted off the road, you could hear the chains a block away. Then they could be taken off until the next snow.

Touch football was played like crazy on this street. At first we only had leather footballs, but you can imagine how long they lasted. Then Dad bought me a new style ball that was made by the Voit Corporation made of a lightweight rubber. That ball lasted forever. When we played touch football, which was every day in the season, the fathers would come out after work or Saturdays and play with us, but they always ended up quarterbacking and calling the plays. Warren and George Huff were the two brothers who usually played with us most of the time.

Tennis baseball was another game we played all summer in the street. We used a regular baseball bat and a tennis ball, no gloves were allowed, telephone poles and markings on the pavements were the bases. As long and hard as we played, we never broke a window, incredible but true. Sometimes we would play at the lower end of the street, next to Lutz's pants factory where Mother worked. There was only one problem. If you hit the ball through the large open windows, and they were all open, you had to go into the factory and were chewed out by one of the bosses. Most of the time I went in and headed straight for my mother and then to Abe Mitman, the manager. He would politely tell me again to play somewhere else.

This was known as a box kite which was more difficult to fly but no challenge was too great when your this gifted.

There were no organized sports in those days, such as Little League Baseball or Midget Football for children, so we organized teams among ourselves. Because this was such an active street, kids from other neighboring streets and sections of town would come and play with us.

Usually in the evenings we would play again in the street, while most parents sat on their front porches with a flyswatter in hand and watched the activity while engaged in conversation with their neighbors. It is amazing what TV did to change all of this. Usually our games changed to kick the can, hide-and-seek, tag, steal the flag, etc. I can still feel the heat and sweat and the fun we had in this wonderful time of our lives.

While growing up on Hughes Avenue, it sounds like all we did was play, and you are right. Our parents, like other parents, gave us very few chores to do. The one thing you learned not to say was, "I'm bored; there is nothing to do" because Mother, in two seconds, found something for us to do.

Did we ever have fights? Yes, but very few. For all the competition in the games, no one ever swore, ever. I can remember only two bad fights I was ever in, each time I came to my brother Paul's rescue. Our parents always told us never to start a fight, but we were to help one another if need be. I was always a big kid for my age, but Paul had a problem with these two boys about four years older than me. I won both fights and handedly and never had a problem with either again.

Another street game that was really fun was called rubber gun fights. We made these guns ourselves by using a piece of wood, cut about twelve inches long and three inches to four inches wide. Then cutting strips of real rubber inner tubes about half-inch wide, we would fasten another piece of wood three-fourths inches wide by six inches long to one end strapping it to the larger body of wood, which became the trigger, and using the other rubber bands, stretched from the front to trigger, which became the bullets. If you got hit with the rubber band, you were dead or out of the game.

BB gun, these words put excitement into every red blooded American boy and fear and turmoil into every parent of a son asking for one. You guessed it, this was me continuing to ask for a Red Rider BB gun. After the war, these guns became available again.

The motion picture Cowboy Red Rider with his young Indian friend, Beaver, were very popular and beside his pistol he carried his trusty rifle holstered to his saddle. Every boy wanted a Red Rider BB gun. I did also but they were hard to get, so when my parents finally gave in after I made a million promises, I got my BB gun, but it wasn't a Red Rider gun and at this point, it didn't matter. I got my gun!

I hate to tell you this next episode, but this book is a true story. Within weeks of using the gun, I headed for the creek and decided to see how powerful this gun was. There were tons of frogs living among the lily pads, there were a few less that day.

This next story shows the immaturity and stupidity of the human race. From time to time you would hear of older kids with their BB guns playing dangerous games with their gun. As far as I know, none of the kids on Hughes Avenue ever did this. First of all, there might have been only one other boy that had a BB gun. Anyway, three or four older boys from another part of town came over to our street looking for more kids to play this game of actually shooting at each other as they hid behind the large trees at Lake Lenape. This was in the autumn so they had light jackets and long pants on. The only rules were you cannot shoot at anyone's head. O' yea, great! It didn't take me more than one half a second to say, not me!

It seemed like every summer we made our racing cars. These were crudely made cars made of wood and any kind of wheels we

Brother Paul and myself with the race car we built with the wheels and axels of an old express wagon. Back yard on Hughes Avenue.

could find, usually off of baby carriages or worn-out express wagons. We did all the work ourselves. They were powered by leg power with one or two kids pushing from behind as we raced them up and down the street.

Another thing that occupied our time was our own carnival that we tried to copy after the Sellersville Fireman's Carnival. We had balls throws to knock down stacked-up tin cans, gambling boards with spinning dials to win nothing. There were no prizes, nothing to win but the thrill of playing at something we enjoyed so much.

Several times a year we would go through a jump rope frenzy. Boys and girls would enjoy this together. Usually you rotated two people to hold and circle the ropes and we would take turns jumping into jump and recite our sayings that kept you in time with the ropes. Double Dutch was spinning two ropes at the same time—you really had to be good to do this. Our parents were not so pleased as we kept wearing out our shoes.

Tramps were very common in this time period, and we had our share on Hughes Avenue. These were homeless men who traveled the country by jumping onto freight trains to do their traveling. They always moved to warmer regions as the seasons changed and lived near the railroad tracks near bridges and tunnels. But to eat, they would come into towns and knock on back doors to ask for food and often ask if there was anything they could do to earn it, which seldom happened. As children, we would see one come into our backyard and ask if mother was home. We would run to the house calling for mother. We were always afraid, but you never heard of any problems. Of course, mother always fed them. They never went into the house, but sat on our back steps as we peeked out the windows to watch.

The Second World War was taking place while we were growing up on the street, and this had a great impact on all of us. We would play army in the fields where the street ended, just below Ketterer's Farm. Here we would dig our foxholes and play our war games. We were also into building what we called forts, which were about four feet to five feet high, made with sticks and wild straw that we gathered from the field and woods.

One day we almost burned the whole field down when someone started a fire in the fort, thinking they could heat the fort because it was late autumn. I was sick at home that day with the flu, but I knew our dad with the other's fathers ran into the field with their brooms and water buckets.

Building model air planes was an exciting past time for many of us kids on the street. These were fighter war planes that we saw in magazines and other war media that we were so proud of. These planes were approximately 18" long with an 18" wing span. They were made with a soft light weight wood called balsa wood glued together to build the body and wings of the plane and then covered with colored tissue type of paper.

It took time and patience but they were great looking and could fly with a propeller that would spin when you wound the rubber band that acted as a motor. It didn't fly far and you better have a wide open space to avoid the crash that will probably happen. I kept my models on my bureau just to look at.

There was an ice cream man who came up the street in the summer about three times a week. This was an old Model T or a Ford-looking station wagon. It had a wooden body that had the side and back completely open so he could work from the inside and dip the ice cream into cones. There were about six flavors that sold for three cents a dip and then moved up in price to five cents. The older kids that earned money could buy two, three, or more dips. The rest of us settled for one.

If our parents forgot to leave money, we would be running to our homes and opening all the places we thought there might be any change lying around. This was a great excitement for us, the moment we heard the bell clang as he turned off Park Avenue and headed up the street. Somehow, I can still smell the ice cream and the cones.

Besides the ice cream man, there were other vendors that plied their wares on the streets. There were butchers and bakers, vegetable hucksters, and an ice man named Mel Bedford who also lived on our street for a time with his family. His truck was a stake body that is a wooden-fenced truck that carried large blocks of ice that he covered with a heavy tarpaulin since there was no roof on the truck. When he would go into a house, we would jump onto the truck and pick up the chips left behind when he chiseled the smaller-size blocks to fit into the iceboxes that actually looked like a refrigerator, except the ice would fit into the upper section, and, of course, this would melt and had to be continually replaced.

We had our icebox until about 1945 or '46 when we got our first electric refrigerator. In a year or two later, the ice man business disappeared forever. There was an ice plant in Perkasie where Prodesco is today, right by the railroad crossing. If Dad needed ice for homemade ice cream, this is where he would go. It was a self-serve plant where you only needed to put a quarter in the machine, and a block of ice would come out from behind a small slide covered with a canvas tarp. We only used the ice plant in warm weather.

In the winter, we used ice from Lake Lenape, especially in the spring when every year the ice that covered the complete creek would break up and flood onto the grounds lining the creek. These were huge chunks of ice about eight inches to twelve inches thick. Dad would take large burlap bag and a hatchet, he would chop the chunks of ice into smaller pieces to fit into the bag, and then using the flat side of the hatchet, he would smash the ice in the bag hitting the outside of the bag to make ice-cubes-size pieces.

We had a hand-churned ice cream machine, and we all would take turns turning the crank handle. Dad had a great recipe; it contained Borden's sweetened evaporated milk, along with the other basic ingredients. He would change the flavors by adding canned fruit. Pineapple was our favorite. We did this in our cellar and usually on a Saturday or Sunday afternoons. We could hardly wait till the machine became very hard to turn because it would be almost done and time to remove the paddle from inside the barrel, and we could put the paddle in a large bowl and clean it off with our own spoons. As you can imagine, this was a happy time.

At the upper end of the street is where we played our army battles in foxholes and straw houses (forts). We also would pick wild strawberries at certain areas outside the young wooded area. At the time school left out, usually the first or second week of June, we knew it was strawberry time. The berries were very small, but very sweet. We took our little tin cooking pots and filled them to the brim. We ate as many picking as we put in our pots. I loved to make strawberry milk by smashing the berries in a glass of milk and stirring them into a perfect blend. Also on my cereal was a delicious treat because the berries were so sweet.

Beyond the woods was the Ketterer's Farm that a few times each summer would go to play in the large barn where they stored hay to feed the cows they raised for milking. This was a large family where the children were grown and mostly married. They also lost a son during the war and had to deal with this difficult time.

Their youngest son, Walter, was a teenager and about five years older than us. He was left to take care of the farm and do the many chores during the day with no one else at home all day because the parents worked in industry at this time. He enjoyed our company whenever we came up. The game we played was using a heavy rope attached to the rafters, and from the hay loft about twelve to fifteen feet from the ground floor, we would swing out on the rope and drop onto a hay wagon loaded with hay. It was really fun and a little risky because you better not miss the wagon when you let go of the rope.

The negative side was it was hot and humid, and if you were ever around hay, it becomes very itchy under these conditions. We couldn't wait to get home and get washed to get relief. It was interesting just to look around the farm and see the cows and chickens with the farm equipment since this was our only exposure to farm life as a child.

The US Gauge now occupies all the farming grounds, so all that's left are good memories.

Where the fields and woods began was where Hughes Avenue ended. This is where this next story took place. Mrs. Stover's house was the last home before the fields began, and this is where, on a cold, early winter day, we saw a skunk. Someone had the great idea to kill this animal knowing the consequences we might be sprayed. There was a pile of unused bricks that we could kill it with. And so we began our pursuit of the skunk.

We started throwing the bricks, but we never hit one time—but the skunk hit me. It was really bad, and I ran home not knowing what my mother would say or could do. As I came into the house, she said get out, get out. I took off my coat and pants on the front porch and then came in. Then up the steps and into the bathtub. No one had showers on Hughes Avenue. My mother washed and washed my clothing using different remedies suggested to her to get rid of the smell.

When about a week later when I used these pants for school, there was only a slight hint of the smell, but when I sat in the hot school room, the smell was really bad, and the whole class started complaining about the smell. The teacher had to send me home to change my clothing and then return to school. That was the last time I wore those pants. The coat evidently was not sprayed as bad, and we were able to save it. I was the only one sprayed that day, but I never saw the tail lifted or the skunk turn around toward me, but I know it happened.

We often would play around Lutz's pants factory and talk to the workers on the ground floor when the large windows were open. We often stood on the cement sills and see who could jump the farthest off the window sills onto the grass. We all made several jumps when I tried to really spring out onto the lawn. I pushed back against the closed window and broke the windowpane with my backside. That ended the jumping contest forever. I don't believe my parents had to ever pay for the pane because as I broke the pane, we all ran away and never came back that summer to that part of the factory. I think I told my mother about what happened but am really not sure.

Everyone had coal furnaces on the street, and all received the coal the same way. A coal truck would park in front of a house and extend a metal coal shoot through your basement window under the front porch. The coal ended up in a coal bin, and then Dad would shovel the coal as needed into the large coal furnace. We had no radiators but a large hole on the first floor with a fancy iron grate that the hot air came through and continued to rise to the second story. On cold winter days, we would stand around or sit around the grate. It felt so good especially coming in out of the cold.

Mother would often dry clothing on a portable wooden clothing rack, placing it right over the grate. It was so comforting, a place to gather around on those long, cold days.

Getting rid of the ashes created by the coal was handled by carrying them out to the alley behind our home and dumping them onto the alley. You would think that the alley would rise six inches a year since all homeowners did the same thing to dispose of ashes, but it never happened. You could hardly notice any change from year to year. Maybe the floods washed them away every year.

When I was eleven years old, I became a paperboy in town delivering the evening *Philadelphia Bulletin* six days a week at 25¢ a day to the grand total of $1.50 a week. I was a backup for the Sunday paper where you got $1.00 for one day, but it was a lot more work because of putting all the inserts together and the heavy load to deliver.

I worked for Jake Esser who owned the business. He was a man in his early seventies with severe diabetes. He could hardly see and lost half of his one foot. He operated the newspaper store at the corner of Main and Temple Avenue, directly across from the Washington House Hotel and on the basement level of the building. He would pass his time playing solitaire cards while waiting for customers.

Reading R.R. Station where we received our bundled newspapers

We—that is, me and two other boys, Robert "Whitey" Clemmer and Arthur "Shorty" Dunlap—would meet at the paper store about 6:00 PM and leave with Gene Erb, another older man about seventy years old, who would be our driver. We served these papers from an old Model T Ford car with canvas roof, no side windows, three half doors, since the right rear door did not exist to make it easy to get in and out of the car. It had spoke wheels and the all-important running boards that someone was always standing on to throw the folded papers onto the porches as we drove the streets.

They had a very good system worked out using three boys. We rotated assignments as we served the town, but our streets and nightly assignments stayed the same. This is what I mean. Starting with the center of town, two of us served the apartment buildings while one boy stayed in the backseat with the bundles of paper to be folded. It was important that enough papers be folded, so as we rotated on the running boards, there were papers to throw. You really had to fold like crazy to keep everyone supplied. With one boy always folding, one on the running boards and then one jumping off and cutting through a yard or alley, you would serve a section of a street by running and throwing your papers. Then you met the car at a designated spot, and you had to be there on time so as not to hold anyone up.

The Cope mansion located about two blocks off Main street on Walnut street. I had to serve this house at the back door. In winter it was dark and scary, I wasted no time at this house. (Courtesy of Sellersville Museum)

We could serve the whole town in forty-five minutes, so you know we were moving. And we did this in all kinds of weather. I broke about two windows in the three years I served papers. Never had to pay but had to ring the door and tell the person what happened. The other boys also broke about the same; it just happened, you know.

When we first arrived to serve, we drove to the train station and waited for the steam train puffing huge billows of smoke from its stack. I can still taste the soot from the smoke. It was a commuter train coming and out of Philadelphia with one car that probably carried US mail. We all had wire cutters to cut the bonding wire on the bundles in back of the car.

Sometimes Gene Erb was not able to drive, especially on Saturday afternoons. Jake, with his very bad eyes, would drive. They were so bad that at every intersection we had to tell him when it was clear of traffic to proceed into the intersection. Main Street always had traffic because Route 309 came through the center of town. It was not rerouted until the 1970s.

Sellersville never got its first red light until the mid-1940s at Main and Park Avenue. We had finally arrived.

Jake eventually sold the business to his son-in-law, Jim Minuccie, from Lansdale. He was also a nice person and I worked for him my last year. Jake was good to us, but he could be a little rough around the edges. Gene Erb was a widower, and he was also a good man and looked out for us as we served our papers. I gave up the papers when junior high football began. I used this money to buy my Schwinn Silver King bike for $79 at Steeley's Gas Station. It was neatest bike in town.

There was a lady living on the street called Mrs. Stover to us, and, by the way, we addressed all adults as Mr. or Mrs. no matter who they were out of respect. Her name was Margaret, and her husband, Paul. They had two grown sons named Charlie and Lee. They had gone into the service during the war. Both were athletic, and Charlie is one of the adults that would play football with us. Lee had a well-known and successful insurance company in Sellersville for many years.

I wanted to give you a little background on her and the family because one person did so much and gave so much to the families by impacting her love on each of us. This was a lady that was involved in the community and especially as she chaired the Republican Club and was a strong Christian. It was a great loss to all when she died in her early fifties. She had a wonderful smile to all, with dark-black hair and was slightly heavy-set in stature.

Every so often in the summers she would call from her front porch, "Ice cream, come and get ice cream."

And we would all come running. She would have a larger container just like the stores would dip from, and she would give it out in cones or plates until it was all gone. We never knew when this would happen, but we always looked forward to it.

The other thing she did every year was have her husband or a neighbor that did not have children dress up as Santa Claus on Christmas Eve and visit every home with children. She would be right by Santa's side and giving an appropriate toy from Santa's bag to every child. These were toys of some value, and we found out later in our lives that she and her husband paid for them all. This just added to an evening that every child was excited about and looked forward to as we looked out our windows, watching Santa go from house to house until he came to ours.

There was one funny episode that happened on Christmas Eve as we were watching Santa across the street. An unmarried young man was doing the honors of playing Santa and had a little too much of the wrong stuff to drink. As he turned around to wave good-bye to the children, he fell completely over the front porch fence and fell at least six feet to the ground. Santa got up and was just fine, and we children were all greatly relieved.

It is people like Margaret Stover that can impact peoples' lives for good by simply showing love and being involved. Hughes Avenue would never be the same without her.

8

All the Holidays

Since I touched on Christmas with Mrs. Stover, I'll give some of my memories of these Christmases from the early and midforties.

Christmas for us children started when the Christmas *Sears Roebuck & Co. Catalogue* would come through the mail in September or early October. We would look and dream and tell Mother exactly what we wanted. We usually got only a few things that we just had to have. Mother did order from the Sears book and also from Fritz's Drugstore in town. Lesher's five-and-dime in Perkasie was always a great place to also visit at Christmas with their decorations and toys on display. There was an aroma in the store that you can never forget. As a boy, I would always head to the section where they had the small lead soldiers and cowboys on their horses and fantasize with them. Mother also purchased our toys there.

Remember there were no malls, no shopping centers, only the local in-town stores to shop in. Life was really different, but every bit as much exciting as it is today and maybe more so.

Hess Brothers in Allentown was a yearly Christmas trip for all of us. This was done on a Saturday, and I cannot describe the excitement and anticipation we felt. Hess Brothers was a huge four-story building with escalators. It would have rivaled Macy's, Gimballs, Lits, John Wanamaker, or any other in Christmas decorations. The store was always winning awards in every category for merchandising.

We got to see children talking to Santa. The lines were always very long, and Mom and Dad did not have time to wait, and we really didn't care either. They had all the toys and the latest toys. The store was jammed. People would line up around the store waiting outside for the store to open and grab the limited advertised specials.

We would have lunch either at a Woolworth, five-and-dime where we sometimes sat on stools at a soda bar, or at a restaurant just off Hamilton Avenue near the Liberty Valley Trolley Station having a hot roast-beef sandwich and french fries.

The city of Allentown was always decorated just beautifully for Christmas, and we would walk the streets in the early evening with the Christmas lights and always freezing temperatures this time of year, but it was all part of the season that made such a mark on our lives.

Christmas in Sellersville began almost about Thanksgiving time when Sellersville started to hang up the lights. Even as a young boy, I always remember the telephone poles being decorated with wreaths, candles, or bells.

Then the stores would begin to decorate, but the homes never did until maybe two to three weeks before. And in our home, the tree was never put up when we were small while we were awake. It was only after we went to bed that Aunt Martha and Uncle Frank were in the house and helped Mom and Dad with the tree. It was put up Christmas Eve and came down New Year's Day, so we only had one week to enjoy it, and that we did.

The houses were decorated very simple in the town. Very few had outside decorations. Most people would hang a lighted wreath the night before Christmas.

Words can never describe the night before Christmas and Christmas morning. When we went to bed, it was so hard to sleep, and then I would wake up during the night and listen for Santa Claus. Can you imagine this! I guess you can because you probably did the same thing. We were warned by our parents no one goes downstairs until they get up. When it was finally morning, we would rush into our parents' bedroom and beg to go down.

When we finally went down the stairs into the living room, it was like a winter wonderland. The tree was lit, the shiny balls and the silver tinsel hanging from the tree branches. Our toys were never wrapped, but they were placed in our own sections and under and around the tree. It was a sight I will never forget. Our parents were very generous to us. They were only average, middle class at this time, but I know we received more than my friends, but, at the time, I didn't think much of it.

There were always Christmas candies in the house like chocolate-filled hard candy, candy canes, and many other Christmas varieties. Mother very seldom had time to bake cookies, but we always had plenty. Probably Aunt Martha baked them; the cutouts were the best. We had Christmas dinner, which took place later in the afternoon and always had Aunt Martha and Uncle Frank with other relatives and Arthur Crouthamel who could be with us.

Another thing I need to point out was that we were at war during the heart of my childhood. The years 1941 to 1945 had a definite effect on Christmas toys and adult presents. From 1943 and '44 you could not buy a metal toy. That's right, no bicycles, no toy guns, no sleds, no skates, no toy cars, and no trucks. Everything was made of paper and cardboard wood. Plastic just was invented and not on the market.

I received a toy pistol made of sawdust glued together and painted silver to look like metal, no moving parts. It lasted maybe a week when the barrel broke off. It was amazing the different toys they did produce with such limited materials to work with. Somehow we understood why and knew the military needed these metals more than we did. One of my prized gifts during the war years was a white navy hat, just like the sailors wore. I was now ready to fight those dirty Japs and Germans.

Christmas music we always looked forward to. We only had our radio to receive music. The stations played very limited music until Christmas Day when they played the music all day and night. We had none of the secular pop songs that came along in the early fifties. The great Christian hymns were sung and only "White Christmas" with Bing Crosby, "Jingle Bells," and the "Christmas Song" with Mel Torme. Rudolph probably arrived about the late forties or early fifties. As children, we knew this music and would sing them at the Christmas parties planned in the town, school, and in church and Sunday school.

Chief "Uncle Mike" Hallman, center, with tax collec-
tor Roland Moyer playing Santa at the party.

Uncle Mike's Christmas party was a big event for the children in Sellersville. About two weeks before Christmas, the Kiwanis Club would sponsor this party that was held at the Moose Lodge, now the American Legion Post on Main Street. This had the largest auditorium in town. Uncle Mike was the chief of police in town for probably twenty-five years. This man was loved and respected by all people, especially us, the children.

Mike Hallman always had a smile for all of us, and our parents upheld him to us. This party is continued today, even though no child remembers him. Another thing about our chief was he never drove his car; his wife had to drive him everywhere he had to go. His office was in the center of town, and his wife was home with his car on Washington Avenue. This was his own car, not a police car. He was a large man and slightly rotund. That added to his friend-to-all appearance.

The party consisted of a short movie, something like *The Three Stooges* of half-dozen cartoons and a comedian that would interact with the children on the stage. Christmas songs and then Santa Claus would give each child a large orange and box of hard candy or chocolate. Our own father played Santa Claus for many years after we were grown and enjoyed it very much as he was a member of the Kiwanis Club.

St. Michael's Lutheran Church. Where I went to Sunday school as a boy.

We were raised in St. Michael's Lutheran Church in Sellersville. Christmas was an important time at the church. The church would be beautifully decorated with a large amount of red poinsettias in the front of it.

The event we looked forward to was the Christmas pageant that we did every year. Rehearsals started about six weeks before Christmas, and I was, at first, a shepherd, then always one of the three kings. The evening we performed the pageant was always exciting, even though there were no speaking parts; just wearing our costumes and doing our parts correctly were enough.

In those days, the borough had raised a large field of Christmas trees in the park system. You would go to the field and simply pick your tree and tag it. Later that week the borough crew would cut and deliver the tree to your door. This is where we bought our trees when I was growing up on Hughes Avenue.

The Heinrick home on South Main Street, directly across from the A&L Restaurant turned their living and dining room into an old-fashioned German Christmas Putz. This was a large platform of miniature village and mountain scenery with moving waterfalls, ski lifts, houses with lights, etc., and always a manger scene. This was always something we went to every year.

We would then walk across the driveway to the DeLancy home where a tree that, at one time could have been a dogwood tree, was painted white and decorated with small gifts wrapped in Christmas paper. There was a gift for every age group and boy or girl. Each was color-coated to identify the gift for you. Inside was a gospel tract also for your age group. Mrs. DeLancy was always careful to remind us to read the tract and don't throw it away. I didn't realize it at the time, but this all had an impact on one that was preparing my heart for my future salvation.

Approximately two thousand people would visit these homes in a season. The six-foot-tall tree is in my brother Paul's possession, since he bought it at auction, and it is still occasionally used for family functions.

The first time I ever bought a Christmas gift was when I was eleven years old. I had money from serving newspapers and bought a bottle of Evening in Paris perfume at Fritz's Drugstore, which was located next to the trolley station on Main Street. I believed Mother was pleased with the gift, and, for the first time, I experienced it was much more blessed to give than receive.

Probably six to eight weeks before Christmas, we would have a family picture taken at Fisher's Furniture Store in Souderton. This picture was only for our family and grandparents, and only in black and white. This promotion brought many families into the store.

New Year's Day was uneventful, mainly because of no television, which meant no Mummer's Parade, or Rose Parade, no football, etc. And, at our age, we never could stay up for the New Year.

Valentine's Day was fun because of buying Valentine cards at Fritz's store or Lesher's in Perkasie and then signing and deciding who to send the best one to in our classroom in school. I always made sure I sent to each classmate.

Easter was another important time in our lives. At this age, it probably was much more secular than spiritual, although I was aware of Christ's death and resurrection. As a child, the Easter bunny and egg atmosphere seemed to dominate.

The Easter candy in stores was available months before in all stores. As a Cub Scout and later Boy Scout, we sold the popular-size coconut and peanut butter eggs by the box. There were twenty-four pieces in a box at five cents an egg. That today would cost probably fifty cents or more.

An interesting episode happened as we were selling at the US Gauge Tavern on Clymer Avenue. Paul, another friend, and I sold a box of peanut butter eggs. The bartender gave us the money and then handed back the eggs to us to enjoy. We were heading for the building called the Scout Shack to play basketball located behind the Heinrich and DeLancy homes back in the fields. We ate the whole box of peanut butter eggs. I got so sick and had to go home. I came so close to throwing up. I could not eat supper. I will never forget the feeling and always respect the power of the egg!

The Sellersville Easter Egg Hunt was a highlight for the children, four years to twelve years old. The Lions Club sponsored the program, which was held at the playground. I took part in it from the time I was in first grade. It was actually a race for the thousands of colored hard-boiled eggs spread over the whole area of the grounds. We were divided into age groups: first to third, fourth to sixth, etc. B. Earl Druckenmiller directed the whole affair with help from the Lions Club. He always could control the huge crowd of children and enjoyed every minute of the proceedings.

We would line up in a straight line with our paper bags or baskets in hand, waiting for the "Get ready, get set, go!" and off we ran, picking up as many eggs as we could. Some of the eggs, maybe one in six, had a prize, such as a large chocolate rabbit. All children received a quarter-pound coconut egg, just for participating in the hunt. It brings back fond memories as I was there from a child, my three children, and most of my grandchildren enjoyed the hunt. It also brings back memories of the men from the Lions Cub who were there, such as Lee Wilhelm, Paul Raushenberger, Ernest Kraft, Harold Gingelsberger, and Nevin Detweiler. All are brought to mind as I reminisce.

We always made a trip to Grammy Duch in Philadelphia for Easter, usually a week before Easter, and Grammy would always make a wonderful meal of fried fish, fried potatoes, etc., with her fantastic receipt of walnut-filled rolled bread. She took the recipe with her when she died. She had baskets of candy for us, and each had a large, solid chocolate standing rabbit. We saw our aunts and uncles at this time, Joe and Kate, Walter and Helen. It was a good time!

In my Sunday best suit in our back yard.

In our home, we usually were outfitted with new Sunday clothes for Easter. I was always hard to buy for since I was such a big kid, not fat, but big. I was eighty-five pounds in first grade. We often would go to Goldbergs in Souderton, and my parents would have to buy men's clothing, and Grammy Clymer would have to adjust the size to fit me. The pants were always knicker pants that stopped below the knee with two-inch-wide elastic bands and socks from the cuff's bands down to your toes. They simply did not have all the sizes for children we have today, and my parents had to pay a lot more for my clothes, but I guess I was worth it—only kidding!

On Easter, as all other Sundays, we were taken to Sunday school by Dad and dropped off. We were picked up afterward or walked home on nice days. Mother never came to church, yet she impacted our lives for good. She taught us right and wrong, love and caring, and every basic teaching taught in Christianity. She was raised Russian Orthodox Catholic Church, which was Grammy Duch's religion, and also Roman Catholic, her stepfather and probably her father's faith. Grammy Duch was very strong in her faith and I believe trusted the Lord as her Savior. On rare occasions, Dad would go to a church service, although more often after 1948.

Memorial Day was a holiday that we looked forward to celebrating each year. Before we had bicycles, we would attend the parade through town with our parents or go on a picnic with Martha and Frank with Grammy Clymer. Once we had our bicycles, we would participate in the parade by decorating our bikes with red, white, and blue cray paper. Just the thrill of driving down Main Street in front of all the people was an experience. Afterward, we would go to the rear of the American Legion Post on Main Street where Rock and Ray's Pizza Place is now located. Here we were treated to hot dogs and sodas. It seemed the sun was always shining that day.

After the war ended in 1945, the parade was enlarged with cars of gold star mothers (mothers who lost their sons during the war) and ranks of soldiers and later the National Guard of the United States unit from Sellersville.

We looked forward to the color guard from the legion when they fired their rifles at the First World War monument, at that time located at Diamond

My bike is all decorated for the parade in town honoring Memorial Day.

and Main Streets. After the soldiers fired the shots in saluting the dead, we would rush out to pick up the shell casings for souvenirs. The memories of the color guard units are still vivid in my mind; they were so smartly dressed and followed each command given them and how in precision they marched. These men never knew the impression they made upon me and our whole community.

Memorial Day with the American Legion at the War Memorial monument at Main and Diamond street.
(Courtesy of Sellersville Museum)

The most interesting thing to happen on Memorial Day was the birth of brother Robert Joseph Clymer, in 1941. A picnic was planned for that day, and we were really excited. There was a small picnic park with amusement rides in Chalfont, Pennsylvania. Mother had prepared the potato salad and other picnic foods the day before. We woke up that morning and all excited to go, when Dad met us in the upstairs hall and said we would not be going because we had a new brother.

Bob was born in our home in the front bedroom and born breech. Dr. Kressley was our family doctor, who lived walking distance away on Diamond Street. We were not happy; we wanted our picnic, but after we were allowed into the bedroom and saw Mother and the baby, we settled down and accepted our fate for the day. We had our picnic in our home with our relatives who were supposed to go with us that day.

Fourth of July celebrated while living on Hughes Avenue, I suppose, was very typical in the community. There were fireworks planned, if not that evening, a weekend before it in Lake Lenape Park. We thrilled to every firework. Compared to today, they were not very good and did not last very long in duration. The small odor given off from the powder can still be smelled today. Honest.

The fireworks we were allowed to handle were the sparklers, the small pack of about twelve cartridges laced together that made a loud bang—it seemed to us—and powder caps used in our cap pistols. That's about all that was allowed in those years.

It was not until we moved off Hughes Avenue that we went to Dorney Park for our Fourth's picnics.

Halloween on Hughes Avenue brings back many memories. There were very few costumes bought in those days. The only thing bought were the faces. There were no rubber masks yet for us to buy. Our costumes started from scratch: hobos, ghosts, witches, football players, cowboys, and everything else that you can imagine. Mother helped us with all of this, gathering and dressing, as most mothers do today, but a lot more work if you only have a mask to start with.

Our first adventure was having a Halloween party at school. This was held in the afternoon, since almost all students went home for lunch unless it rained or snowed. The lunch hour was one hour. They must have given us a longer lunchtime that day. We came back dressed in our costumes, and a party in each class was held. In our school-rooms, we would learn Halloween songs and poems that added to the excitement in school and the holidays in general. I still remember a song we learned in third or fourth grade. The words are as follows:

The brownies one night told the fairies to come to their Halloween ball, to be given the last of October when Jack

Frost had made all the leaves fall. The crickets would furnish the music, the fireflies would furnish the lights, the toadstools would furnish the setting, and all be a beautiful sight.

It had a lovely melody. If you listen closely, you can still hear it.

Halloween night was always a moonlit evening, not too cold, just a little cool with leaves lying on the pavement and gutters. There were about eight large maple trees that lined the street and produced all the yellow leaves as they fell to the ground. We had one in our front yard, which left very little grass grow there because of the shade it produced.

Remember this was a friendly, family-oriented street. Every house on the street participated in inviting all of us into their homes, and all gave candy and sweet gifts. Five-cent candy bars that now cost fifty cents or more today was a favorite, along with candy-coated or caramel-coated apples. Many homes gave Halloween-decorated napkins filled with candy corn, pretzels, cookies, etc., and then the four corners were folded together to the center and tied together with a rubber band.

We tried to get to as many homes as we could so we would have a load of goodies when we went home. There were twenty homes on Hughes, so our goal was to complete the street and move on to Park Avenue, and then the bottom part of Diamond Street, which we very seldom accomplished.

The most frustrating thing to us was when people could not guess who we were and kept us there it seemed forever. The idea, of course, was to make people guess who you were. Finally they would give up, and you took off your mask to show yourself and tell your name. We only had so much time to cover our territory that evening, and we wanted all the candy we could get in our paper bags. It was a good time for us as children to get into homes and meet, especially the neighbors we were not familiar with.

What I am about to write now I am not proud of, but I wish to share because this was part of Halloween experience. I never told my children or grandchildren about this until they were grown up, because I would never want them to use it as an excuse to do something as stupid.

Mischief night was the night before Halloween. We were allowed to be out this evening because we had field corn that we saved from neighboring farms and would throw the kernels on people's porches and front doors, then run away when they turned the porch lights on. We had the bright idea to harass a man and wife who lived on Park Avenue and just around the corner from Hughes Avenue. These people never would open their home on Halloween, and we remembered this.

So we threw our corn, hard and long, and no response, so next we pulled out all the flowers, like mums and then small shrubbery and dirt from their garden and threw all this on their front porch. Well, this got their attention, and we all ran, but one of the kids called out my name as I was climbing over the four-foot high wire fence in the backyard.

Of course, the people heard it and hollered back, "We're calling the police."

And sure enough, they did. Well, we all ran home, and I never said a word to my mother. Dad was at work and not home. I was scared stiff, and then the knock on the door with big Chief Mike Hallman standing there, I actually evaporated into thin air at this point. This is what I wanted to do. Mother knew nothing, so I had to explain to both at the same time and had to give names of the other children.

Chief Hallman gave me and Paul a stern talking to, and we promised never to do this again. I was embarrassed to tell my mother and then to Dad when he came home. We never got a spanking, just another talking to from both. We had to go back that night and apologize to these neighbors. They were very gracious and asked us why, and I told them the truth. Their home was open on Halloween night from then on.

The last holiday we celebrated was Thanksgiving Day. This was still the period in time before television, so again no Santa Claus parades or football games on TV. Sell-Perk High School played at ten thirty on that morning as Pennridge currently carries on the tradition.

I know we went to some of the evening games, but I don't remember one on Thanksgiving Day. We mainly just hung around the house, waiting for the dinner that Mother was preparing. We always had Aunt Martha and Uncle Frank, along with Arthur Crouthamel or a relative who lived with us after Arthur died.

Thanksgiving and Christmas we always had turkey or chicken. We very seldom had these birds during the rest of the year; it was always beef or pork. The reason I mention chicken is because Dad was busy as he was working at his job. He also did handyman work for Dr. Kressley on Diamond Street. He would do simple repair work around the house, even built a set of cement steps used by all patients using his office. The other thing I remember was killing chickens for him. Dr. Kressley had his own chicken coop with almost two dozen chickens that laid eggs.

Dr. C.A. Kressley our family doctor for all my childhood years. A gifted man and physician. (Courtesy of Sellersville Museum)

When he dressed chickens, always about three at a time, Dad could keep one for himself. This is how we would sometimes have one at Thanksgiving. These were large chickens. I would always watch as Dad and Arthur would go about their work. Dad would catch one at a time from the large chicken coop into a burlap bag, take it out behind the garage, and, with his axe, while holding the legs with the other hand, would chop off the head, and the bird would always flap its wings so wildly, it would fly out of his hand, take about twelve steps and fall over without his head.

Then they put the whole chicken in boiling water and pull out all the feathers and then gut the chicken. Dad did this maybe two or three times a year. Dr. Kressley was a fine doctor for his time. He was a distinguished-looking man, probably in his early fifties. I remember going to his office and you never needed an appointment. There was no such thing as that; you simply went to the office and waited for your turn. A visit cost $3 or less, and you always got your medications at the same time from him. He made house calls like all doctors and delivered Robert and David in our home.

Doctors would come to your house to treat you. You simply had to make a phone call, which we never had a phone while living on Hughes Avenue. Mother or dad would go to a neighbor who had a phone and there were only a few on the street. Aunt Martha, dad's sister, did have a pone but it was a party line phone which means you shared a line with maybe 2, 3, 4 or more people who could actually listen in on your phone call. Well, we needed some excitement!

Getting back to Dr. Kressley, he would come as soon as time would allow because he also made his hospital calls. He carried a black satchel bag where he carried his stethoscope, pills, etc. This practice continued until the late fifties or early sixties.

Dad took me to Dr. Kressley once when I had flu-type symptoms. I had to wait in the waiting room for a little while and was really feeling sick. Finally it was my turn, and the doctor saw me. The problem was I had to throw up really bad, and Dad and the doctor were in a conversation and wouldn't let up. Finally we left the office, and, as soon as I hit the steps that Dad actually built, I let loose all over them and the pavement. But no sooner after I vomited I began to feel well. Dr. Kressley never knew how close he was to losing his office that day.

Dad became such good friends with him that he took our whole family to his cabin in the Pocono Mountains for a weekend. Yes, I still remember much about that trip. He shared his favorite chocolate cake recipe with Mother that she used forever. I remember the secret ingredient was mayonnaise.

When Barry was born in 1947, he was born in Grand View Hospital, as was my brother Jerry. Mother was set on calling him Jack. But that was the name of Dr. Kressley's German shepherd dog, and, as children, we persuaded Mother not to call him after a dog. She called him Barry, and we were all happy. His baby nickname was Bambi since Walt Disney's movie by that name was the great movie of the year.

I mentioned Arthur Crouthamel and others who lived with us. In fact, I don't remember a time when someone was not living with us.

Arthur was a difficult name for us to pronounce, so we knew him as Arto. He moved from the Green Street row house where he had a room since his wife died. This was his only place that he could live and board at this time. When my parents bought their home on Hughes Avenue, Arthur asked to move in with them, and they accepted. Arto was a retired cigar maker with nothing more to live on than his Social Security, which was very little in those days. I really don't think Mom and Dad made any money on the deal, because he ate with us, and Mother did his wash and ironing.

Arthur Crowthamel and Dad in our back yard. Arthur lived with us our first seven years on Hughes Ave.

Arto was old at the time, probably around seventy. He walked with a cane, chewed tobacco, smoked a few cigars, and liked beer whenever possible. He never had any children, but he was good to us. He was less-than-average height with rotund waist. We loved when he would read our children stories and nursery rhyme books to us, as we would climb on his large stuffed chair and crowd around him. He always had bags of candy available for us.

Apples were bought by Dad by the bushel baskets, usually at the Q-Mart or door-to-door hucksters, so we had plenty of them. Arto would peel them for us and cut them through the center to check for worms because half of the apples had them. There was no pesticide sprays at that time. He walked Paul and me to a barber on Clymer Avenue whose name was Clemmer, the first house on the row houses. Then, on the way home, he would stop at the Gauge Tavern to have a glass of beer.

I would walk with him when he would go to Nolan's Cigar Factory at Maple and Branch Streets, which is now replaced with an apartment building. He would buy his chewing tobacco there in a large paper shopping bag. This meant he also had a spittoon in our home where he spit his tobacco juice. He raised his own horse radish in our small backyard and gathered more of it that grew behind Buck's Furniture Store and then grind it into a spread. Another habit of his was to eat limburger cheese on crackers, but he had to eat it only in the basement because it smelled so bad. Our sister, Anna, loved it also, and both would go down to eat it.

He lived with us during the war years, and he and Dad would talk and listen to Gabriel Heater and the news every night on the radio. They always had a bottle of Stegmaier Gold Medal beer made in Allentown to drink while listening to the news. Sometimes I also had a small shot glass of it, which I never thought anything of because Dad had it. Gabriel Heater always started the program with "There is good news tonight" even if it wasn't true. This was always the highlight of the day.

Arto's death was a new experience for all of us. We knew he had a heart problem and was doctoring for it. But there was no medicine and tests to help people; you just lived out your time. I don't know if he was a believer. He never went to any church. The only thing I remember that happened in the spiritual realm was when we came home, probably after Grammy Duch. I know we were away overnight, and when we arrived home, Arto, I believe, was drinking in his room, and we could hear him praying a prayer calling out to God for forgiveness, etc. He was loud and sounded sincere. He also had the Pennsylvania Dutch accent, as so many older people had at that time.

Arthur died while he slept on a November evening in 1944. We woke up in the middle of the night, it seemed, although it probably was closer to morning. I know it was dark, and Dr. Kressley was there already to pronounce him dead. We heard the talking and came downstairs because his door was closed, and at that point, we did not know anything. We saw Mother was crying, and she told us Arto died. She said we could go to his room to see him. I will always remember standing there and then touching his hand and how cold it was. We weren't afraid; it was a new experience to have someone die in your home and view this person.

The funeral was at Wilhelm's Funeral Home. Arthur had only one relative and the wife at the funeral. Paul Truague and his wife, friends of Mom and Dad and our family, were the only ones at the home. The pastor from Jerusalem Lutheran Church conducted the service. Paul and I got into a laughing jog during the service, and we were on the front row and separated by Mom and Dad. We would lean forward and look at each other and start laughing. Mom and Dad saw us, and we were sure there was going to be two more funerals that day after Mother looked at us.

We went to the cemetery at the Almont Jerusalem Church where he is buried next to his wife in unmarked graves. I've been back there several times but never found the gravesites. It was bitter cold that day and gray skies that turned into snow as the gravesite service was concluding. There was no money to bury him, so he had only what Social Security could provide. The casket was cloth-covered, and the outside box was wood.

Paul received Arto's gold pocket watch because Arto told Mother he was to have it because Paul liked to listen to the ticking of the clock. I received the penknife that was used to peel all those apples we enjoyed him peeling for us. I still think of him from time to time and how Mom and Dad reached out to help people more than they ever knew.

Uncle Joe, Mother's brother, came to live with us for a short time, around 1940-1941. Uncle Joe was a happy-go-lucky fellow. We loved him, and he always showed love to us. He came to live with us because in Philadelphia, there was little work to be had, so Dad gave him a job at Green Tweed in North Wales. Uncle Joe slept in the same room with us since Arto had the back room. He looked much like Liam Neeson, the movie star.

Uncle Joe made friends easily. He loved his beer drinking with his buddies. He played football with the Sellersville Greenjackets team, and when living in Philadelphia, he was a club boxer, and I believe pretty good. He was strong, athletic build, full head of black hair, and could move quickly with a slightly bent nose from boxing.

He loved to go fishing at Lake Lenape. I remember when I learned at this young age that Uncle Joe was going to join the army. This decision, I believe, was made just before or right after we went to war. I believe it could have been before because I remember the weather being warm when I heard it. Pearl Harbor was December 7, 1941. The second reason was brother Bob would be born, and the house was shrinking. Bob's middle name is Joseph. Thank you, Uncle Joe.

Uncle Joe visited us only a few times during the war, and we were always excited to see him come while he was being trained. He told us the army did not even have enough uniforms when he first joined. He was sent to Newfoundland and then to Europe. I don't know where he fought, except it was the Germans. He refused a promotion to sergeant because he didn't want to be above his new buddies he made. He saw a lot of fighting, but never talked about it. He gave me all his medals after the war, and somehow I lost them all. I would love to know something about the story of his war record.

He married a lovely blonde German girl after the war, and I can still hear Mother saying, "How did you ever marry such a nice person?"

Joe would always have an answer. Kate was her name. She brought her mother and other family members over to Philadelphia. A nephew became a veterinarian in Philadelphia.

She told us that as a child, she was selected to give a bouquet of flowers to Adolph Hitler. She told us of the hardships the civilians suffered during the war and how the population knew when Hitler invaded Russia. They could not win the war, but no one could speak against it. Joe and Kate never had children, although I believe they might have had a baby daughter in Germany that died. Joe died around 1972 from a stroke, and Kate, a year later of a brain tumor. They were only in their late forties or early fifties.

After Arthur died, a young teenage girl came to live with us named Mildred Fluck. We needed a responsible person to watch us while Mother had to work to support our family. Fortunately, it was just down the street to Lutz's pants factory. Mildred was about sixteen years old with no parents. Her mother had just died, so she was living with her older sister. She had quit school, and Mother needed someone here at the home when she left early for work. It was a perfect fit. She seemed much more mature for her age and was a larger body size, not fat, just strong.

Mildred was good to us and a good children sitter. She had a very strong Pennsylvania Dutch accent in her speaking. She loved the movie cowboys, as Gene Autry, Roy Rogers, Red Rider, Lone Ranger, and Tonto. Since there was no television yet, Dad would drive us to the Plaza Movie theater in Perkasie. Bernard Haynes was the owner. Usually Mildred and I would take the trolley from the station on Main Street, across from the firehouse and take it to the Perkasie Station on Walnut Street, now the American Legion. Monday and Tuesday nights were double features and usually had the cowboy movies or Saturday afternoon, so these are the days we could go. Twenty-five cents was the ticket price, and I think the trolley was about the same.

Mildred must have been dropped off in the morning because David was born at home in 1942, and I know she was with us at this time because she wanted Mother to call him Gene for his middle name, but Mom didn't care for it and called him David Eugene. I mentioned she was cowboy crazy, and Gene Autry was her favorite. It wasn't until after Arthur died that she actually moved in with us and lived with us until about 1945-1946. She remained friends with our family throughout her life. She married Harold Bergey several years after leaving us to work in a pants factory, and both she and Harold died within a year of each other with no children, but had some infants that died.

When Mildred left us, another young teenage girl came to sit us. She never lived with us, but was with us all day. She was only about thirteen or fourteen years old. Again, she was much more mature for her age and had a take-charge spirit and knew how to take care of children, since she was also from a large family from South Perkasie. Her name was Mary Knitter, and we all liked her very much. She was good to us, but strict in discipline. She always followed Mother's orders.

Because Mother worked so close to home, she would run home at lunch, and we would have lunch with her since we would walk all the way home from school, with one-hour lunch. Then Mother would start supper or give clear orders to the sitters for our suppers. There was never a time we went without dessert at every meal. Dessert was always something from the bakery. We had two bakers stop almost every day and then at the grocery store. Dad loved a bun at breakfast with his cereal. Somehow we all got that gene in us. After school, there were Tastykakes in the bread box or other cakes before supper. We were really privileged children, but never really appreciated it until after grown and could look back at how our parents loved and sacrificed for us.

Mary was with us until we moved from Hughes Avenue to Green Street. She also worked in a pants factory and married, had one or two children, and, as of this writing, is fighting MS.

When Mildred left us around 1945-1946, Mother's sister Aunt Rose came to live with us. She had worked at the Navy Yard during the war, but when it ended, so did most of the jobs, so she also came to live with us and work for Dad. She was also good to us and enjoyed the few short years she lived with us. She did very little sitting since that area of our lives was already taken care of with Mary Knitter. I always had a close relationship with Aunt Rose. She would take us children into town and buy us ice cream sundaes at Shelly's Ice Cream Store.

One Christmas 1947 or 1948, Aunt Rose took me with her to downtown Philadelphia for Christmas. This was a day I will never forget since it was my first time into that part of the city. There was so much to see, and the city was decorated for Christmas. We visited most of the big department stores. There were no malls; everyone shopped the stores. One of the highlights was eating at Horn and Hardart restaurant where you put change into the different food stations. The little door opens, and you take your food. It was very popular at that time.

The other surprise of this trip was Aunt Rose telling me I could pick out my Christmas present. Well, the one thing I wanted that year was a real football helmet, which she bought me. It looked like a University of Michigan helmet with the Michigan colors. No face bars, only hard leather, not plastic. This is what we had in those days, but I was proud and happy and couldn't wait to use it.

Aunt Rose met and married a Second World War veteran named Russell Ruth. He was of Mennonite background but went against his church and parents' beliefs to be a pacifist and joined the US Army. He was very seriously wounded in the Battle of the Bulge. He walked

Mother's sister Aunt Rose with sister Anna at Lake Lenope.

with a slight limp, and I saw his bullet wounds in his stomach and chest when at the shore swimming. They had one child, Barbara, and then divorced after about six years of marriage. Aunt Rose was Roman Catholic and even took me to St. Agnes RC Church in town several times. This was in the small original building.

Later in her life, after Barbara became a born-again Christian, Aunt Rose was led to saving faith in Christ by Barbara. I visited her just a few days before she died in Grand View Hospital, which I will never forget as she shared with me her feelings to me as a young boy and as I grew into manhood. We worked many years together with Dad at Industrial Safety Clothing, which Dad was co-owner of in Sellersville. We were on different floors, but I would see her every day.

The last family member from Mother's family to live with us was Uncle Walter, who never lived with us on Hughes Avenue, but when we lived on Green Street. He also came to work for Dad because of lack of work in Philadelphia. We enjoyed him being with us. He also played Greenjackets football as a running back. Walter would go back and forth to Philadelphia on many weekends where he met his first wife and moved back to be with her and be married. He also fought in the Second World War, but fought against Japan and fought in the Philippines.

His marriage ended in divorce, but he remarried and had a son that he was so proud of. He died in his midsixties caused by a brain tumor. He, like all Mom's siblings, loved our family, and we always enjoyed seeing each other, which if they didn't live with us only saw each other several times a year. Upon his death, his ashes were spread in the ocean at Wildwood, New Jersey, where they owned a mobile home and spent their free time there. He was Roman Catholic.

9

Second World War

The Second World War, as I experienced it and now look back, was fascinating to say the least. This war was different from any other wars I have experienced the rest of my life. This war was a war that consumed everyone completely in everything you did and thought. This was a war that had to be won. Our whole nation was geared to a must win; there was no other way. I will touch on how it affected my life, our family, and country.

A very interesting story took place on our street early in the war years. There was a family with three boys that had strong ties to the German Nazi Party. In the summers before the war, the two older boys would train at the German American Bund camp outside of Sellersville. They called it the Deutschhorst Country Club. It was in operation for two years as a social club for German American people where they could drink their German beer, eat their German food, danced, and hold shooting contests and sporting events. But the underlying reason was to promote the Nazi Party, glorify Adolph Hitler, and promote the Arian race and anti-Semitism. It is believed this property was actually purchased by a German spy.

It was located in a beautiful country setting with an old stone mill building as the headquarters and social meetings along the Branch Creek.

The other very important aspect for the club was a camp where they would train boys from eight to sixteen years old to become soldiers. They were trained with rifle practice as well as all the other necessary training military men would use. Worst of all was the indoctrination of these youths to the Nazi propaganda—all the time using the American flags to disguise their real agenda. They recruited boys from Philadelphia to Allentown, Pennsylvania. Fortunately, very few came out of Sellersville and neighboring communities.

This all came to a climatic end when a large rally was held with two thousand of the faithful gathered. Two newspapers were there, the Allentown *Morning Call* and the *Sellersville Herald*. During the rally, The *Morning Call*'s camera, was confiscated, but Robert Baum's camera was not, he was the son of Walter Baum, and the pictures and story about the bund camp exposing who they really were was all printed. Once the local citizenry heard and saw this, they were outraged. The Sellersville American Legion actually went in and raided the club. A short time later, the state police moved in and closed the club and camp.

But the story did not end for us on Hughes Avenue. Before the camp was closed, the boys would come home with scratches on their faces from training in the woods and then practice their goose step marching in the street. My mother said I and other neighbor children would also join with them, but I have no recollection of this.

The father was employed at the US Gauge company, one of the largest producers of gauges in the United States. Our father told us one night the state police came in and arrested him and moved the whole family out of their home. As children, we couldn't understand how they were there one day and gone the next. He was arrested for having or planning to make explosives in his garage that could have been used in the Gauge Company.

The 1930s witnessed the rapid growth of the aircraft industry, and the US Gauge participated in this growth by developing and producing altimeters, airspeed indicators, compasses, oil and manifold gauges, and fuel pressure indicators for the expanding market. When the Second World War began, they became a major supplier for the aircraft industry. The company and employees were awarded the Army-Navy "E" for excellence in 1944 by our country.

They employed two thousand people and were protected with very tight security even a high barbed-wire fence.

As children, we would stand outside the barbed-wire fence, and in the summer with their windows open, we would beg for the workers to throw over the fence some of the dial indicators for us to take home to make games where we could fasten and spin these dials. They often would do this and tell us, "Now go home!"

Once again, little Sellersville, in a strange way, is touched by the war and plays its part in the greatest generation, and I experienced it.

I mentioned in the introduction about the very unusual amount of generals that came out of a 2,500 population living in Sellersville at that time. There is a total of five men that achieved that rank.

Brigadier General Henry Delp Styer was commanding officer of American Expeditionary Forces in Siberia in the First World War. Major General Howard A. Gilkeson was a graduate of West Point and an aviation pioneer. Two brothers attained the rank of brigadier generals, General H. Alvin Cressman and brother Louis G. Cressman.

Brigadier General Hugh Niles achieved his rank after the war. He was a B-24 bomber pilot during the war and flew thirty-five missions into Europe. He joined the Pennsylvania National Guard in 1953. Eventually he became chief of staff at headquarters in Indiantown Gap and then went on to become a general.

Hugh Niles actually lived on Hughes Avenue for a few years after the war while I was still a boy living there. When I became an adult, we became friends, and I got to know the man he was. He was patriotic beyond anything you could imagine, with a great sense of humor that easily gained him friends and a person that could get things accomplished. After he retired, he

Brigadier General Hugh Miles

involved himself in community affairs and politics and was honored by the Bucks County Republican Committee for his years of service.

Here is a story about this man: When we moved to Green Street from Hughes Avenue, Hugh also moved there. We were now young teenagers and needed a basketball court. Somehow, he got involved and got Pennsylvania Power and Light, who had a work crew in Sellersville, to donate two used poles. The neighbors chipped in some money for the baskets and nets, but Hugh actually did the work and brought our court to reality. Thank you, General Niles!

A well-known and respected surgeon from Sellersville also enlisted in the navy and had the rank of captain. He was Dr. Clyde R. Flory, with offices in Sellersville.

Pearl Harbor, of course, began the war, but I do not have any recollection the day it happened. I knew about it a short time later because every adult was talking about the bombing. Dad was always of the opinion that Roosevelt purposely left the Japs bomb Pearl Harbor so America would be forced into it.

Russell Shelly, Jr.

Russell Shelly, better known to everyone as Ziggy, was our plumber and lived next to Dr. Kressley on Diamond Street. His son joined the navy and played in a band on one of the battleships that sunk. That ship was the battleship *California*. His son was killed in the attack that day. It was his only son, and Dad said he was a very likeable boy who would go out on jobs and help his dad and the men working there. Our little community was affected from the very beginning.

The Shelly family would be the first of many in the town that would be displaying a special banner in their front door or window showing that they had a son or daughter serving in the military. This banner was approximately eight inches wide by twelve inches long; red, white and blue; a wooden dowel across the top with a gold cord to display it. Every member serving was represented with a monogrammed silver star and, if they sacrificed in battle, a new flap with a gold star representing their death.

I am not sure how to capture the pride and spirit felt in America and experienced in our community to win this war. We were all united. The war was talked about every day and probably many times a day. The news media, radio, movies, churches, schools, factories—you name it, the war was there.

As a community, many men and women enlisted or were drafted. Many of the young men even quit school to join the military, and we lost some of these young people who gave their lives for such a noble cause. As individuals, many are forgotten; as a group, we can never forget their sacrifice for us. Between the communities of Sellersville and Perkasie, seventeen young men paid the ultimate sacrifice for their country.

*The Spirit of Sell-Perk B17 bomber purchased by
our communities of Sellersville and Perkasie*

We, as a community joined with our good neighbors in our sister town Perkasie, sacrificed financially to purchase a B-17 bomber for the US Army Air Force named *Spirit of Sell-Perk*. It seemed whatever our government asked of us, it was never too much. This was always the attitude in our home as well as the attitude for all my young friends.

This bomber project was a great community uniter because we could physically see, by buying war bond stamps, what our money was actually buying and to see your communities name on it was very gratifying.

The bomber cost 450,000.00 dollars. The amount raised was 2,000.00 dollars over this amount. The students of the Sell-Perk school system set this goal and raised it beating the time they also set to do this by one day. June 1, 1944 was the day all the money was raised. These numbers are staggering because we are talking 1944 when people were only earning 45.00 to 75.00 dollars a week. The words to describe this achievement is love and sacrifice for our country. The school children by popular vote named the plane as we know it the "Spirit of Sell-Perk".

John Rivers

John Rivers was an orphaned Native American boy placed in the home of Mr. and Mrs. Elvin Horne in a neighboring community named Appelbachsville but was always upheld as one of us. He was an outstanding football player and amateur boxer and turned professional before the war. He also played football for the Sellersville Greenjackets amateur football club. His parting remarks to the well-known sports coach and personality in our community, B. Earl Druckenmiller, was a prophetic forecast of his death: "I might not make it out of the war, but I'll take many with me."

John was twenty-three years old when he was killed at Guadalcanal in the Pacific in 1942. He was awarded the Navy Cross for heroism along with his other metals, including the Purple Heart.

John was a machine gunner in the First Marine Division at the Battle of Tenaru River. Outnumbered ten to one and overrun, he killed over two hundred enemy soldiers all in one night. This was attested to by his ammo carrier, Al Schmidt of Philadelphia, and gun commander corporal, Lou Diamond of Brooklyn, New York.

A Hollywood movie was made of John and the marines in this battle. The 1945, Warner Bros. filmed *The Pride of the Marines*. Actor Anthony Caruso played the role of John Rivers in the film. Al Schmidt was seriously wounded and blinded by a hand grenade but continuously kept firing the machine gun and was also credited for killing two hundred Japanese soldiers. Out of eight hundred Japanese soldiers, only fifteen survived.

John Rivers was a full-blooded American Indian. His mother died when he was an infant. Along with two sisters, they were placed in the Lutheran Orphans' Home and Asylum in Philadelphia and at age fourteen was placed with Mr. and Mrs. Elvin Horne. John was buried at Guadalcanal island in August 1942.

In our home, the name Johnny Rivers was constantly mentioned throughout the war and after. He was a role model for everyone, a very likeable, decent, moral young man who overcame great obstacles and achieved success although it was short-lived. But it was the impact he made, which lasted till this day.

All the young men, eighteen years to thirty-five years, were eligible for the draft. There were at least a half dozen on our street who either joined a service branch of their choosing or were drafted. Milt Minninger, who had about four or five children, joined the marines since he served there before and didn't want to chance being drafted in the army. This was difficult for this family to go four years without their dad.

Our own father repaired our leather shoes by resoling and heeling them as needed. He would use shoe nails and a steel mold to bend over the nails. We would always need a new liner to keep the nails from our feet. He would do the same thing for this family for the length of the war. I don't know how he managed to do all these things, but he did.

A note of interest, after the war, Mr. Minninger learned the trade of repairing shoes and opened his own repair shop for some years next to Frederick's Barbershop.

Dad was never going to be drafted for several reasons. First, he was in his early to mid-thirties. Second, he had four to five children and, most importantly, his status as supervisor in production for 1-A related companies, which was making asbestos gloves and clothing for steel corporations. He knew early on that the company he worked for put him in this classification and would keep him out.

In fact, all my friends' fathers were never drafted. They were about my dad's age, but they all worked at the US Gauge Corp. located in Sellersville, and that might have kept them out of the draft.

Mother worked at Lutz's pants factory at the bottom of Hughes Avenue. They employed about one hundred people at this time and manufactured exclusively military pants. This was typical for all manufacturing during the war. Only a small percent was allowed for civilian purchasing.

Security at the Gauge plant was very tight. You had a photo badge if you were employed there; police protection was around the clock. The plant was protected with a barb-wire hurricane fence. There were two thousand people working at the Gauge, and it was probably the largest gauge plant in the United States at the time.

About a half mile south on Diamond Street was an erected lookout airplane spotter tower made entirely of wood. It was about three or four stories high and stood at the crest of a hill. It was believed this was for spotting German planes that could bomb the plant.

Air-raid drills were held about once a month or once every two months. They were held during the evening and were unannounced. Air-raid wardens were usually older men who volunteered to police their neighborhoods being sure no lights were on. All people had to pull their shades, etc. If anyone did not cooperate, their door was knocked on and could be fined. There was never a problem though because people all obeyed the laws.

This was always a scary time because the fire sirens would blow for a long time, and we never knew if it could be for the real thing.

The lights would be out, but Dad would turn on our Farnsworth floor model radio, which brother Paul has in his possession. The small amount of light that came from the dial was just enough to be able to relax us until the all-clear sirens would end the drill.

Air-raid drills also were practiced during the day, but no sirens were sounded. Daytime drills were for the schoolchildren in the schools. We would be taken from our classrooms in the Sellersville elementary schools on Church Street and taken into homes on Green Street and High Street. People with usually a mother at home had arranged for as many as a dozen children to enter and wait for ten to fifteen minutes and then walk back to our classes in orderly fashion. The reason being the enemy would mistake the large buildings for factories and not so with the smaller homes.

Within the classroom, we also practiced hiding under our desks in case we could not leave the building. All the glass panes in the rooms were protected from breakage by Scotch tape holding the glass together in case of a bombing. The tape was placed diagonally from corner to corner, then directly through the center vertically, and on center horizontally. This was what we looked at every day, a constant reminder of the war.

War bond stamps were sold every week for twenty-five cents a stamp and then pasted in your war bond book. This was a challenge to fill your book as quickly as possible. After you paid about $18 and some change, your book was worth $25.

Another way to fill up your bond book was the steel scrap drives at the schools. This was really exciting because you earned money on all steel scrap you brought to the school grounds on a given day. A scale was set up to weigh the scrap, and there was also a military vehicle on the grounds manned by army soldiers. We would scour our basements, relatives' houses, and gas station's trash piles—anywhere we could find scrap. Dad would bring home an old, worn-out sewing machine for me to take on our express wagon to school. It would be weighed and then thrown on the huge scrap pile, and the following week I was given the stamps.

The Sellersville Cemetery was once enclosed with a large iron-post fence. This was donated for the war effort. Again, everything was on the line to ensure victory for the United States.

Rubber was another item needed and was in short supply that the government would buy from citizens.

Going to the movies in Perkasie was a patriotic experience. Before the movie started, for fifteen minutes to half an hour, you could hear the news on the radio played before the show because people wanted to hear the war news. Then we all stood up and sang the national anthem while the music and flag were displayed on the screen. Every night before the main film started, they showed a ten-minute war film on a fighting somewhere in Europe or the Pacific Theater. Even though it was a probably a month old, we craved to see the real action, and it was always positive even when things were not going well. Movie stars were drafted, or they volunteered for duty and many saw action. Those left behind went out on bond drives and were actively supporting the war effort.

Music was a great motivator in supporting our military. Even the big bands like Glenn Miller incorporated marches into their performances, such as the march "American Patrol. He joined the service and had his own band to support morale. He lost his life while flying to one of those assignments.

Great love songs were written like "I'll Be Seeing You" (in all the old familiar places), "I'll Never Smile Again" (until I smile with you), "Don't Sit Under The Apple Tree" (with anyone else but me). Every love song ever written took on special meaning to those serving and those left behind.

And then there were the songs written to promote morale that as kids we especially enjoyed even as we played. Such as "Praise the Lord and Pass the Ammunition" (all aboard we're not going a fishing), "You're in the Army Now" (you're not behind a plow, you'll never get rich by digging a ditch, you're in the Army now), "Coming in on a Wing and a Prayer". The song to promote War Bond sales, "Any Bonds Today" (bonds are freedom and this is what we're sellling, any bonds today), and, of course, the great Andrew Sisters song "Boogie Woogie Bugle Boy".

ing, any bonds today), and, of course, the great Andrew Sisters song "Boogie Woogie Bugle Boy".

And, last but not least, our wonderful patriotic songs that took on new meaning because our loved ones were dying and paying the ultimate price for their country. I remember as a young boy standing with pride singing about our country and the armed forces songs. "America the Beautiful", what an inspirational song. "God Bless America" made famous by Kate Smith with a story on this song. Kate needed a patriotic song, so she went to Irving Berlin and asked what he had. He said he wrote this song years ago but didn't think much of it. Well, now you know the rest of the story. And then our great "National Anthem" that rang in the heart of every American.

Great love songs were written. Christmas was especially sentimental because of sadness of lives lost or wounded and just being separated. I can remember much of this music on the radio and still sense the things I just mentioned.

The motion picture industry made many films about the war and motivated all of us to keep fighting the enemy and inspire young men to join and fight in the military.

Dad was in charge of the production at Green Tweed Glove and Clothing Manufacturing during the war, which at the time employed sixty people. The young men who worked there usually came to Dad to get his opinion on which branch of the service they should join or just wait to be drafted.

His opinion was always the navy. The main reason was you always know where your bed is, and you know where your next meal is coming from. Some took his advice, and some didn't, of course, but the one thing that didn't change was they remained friends throughout the war, and some stayed friends in their whole lifetime.

With all the responsibilities to raising us children, they always, both Mom and Dad, would write and receive the letters from these men. It was interesting to see the letters coming from these men because every, yes, every letter, was read by people hired by the government to make sure no security information was passed on even innocently to wrong people. You knew this because some sentences were blocked out in every letter—incredible, but true.

These same men would always come to visit Dad, sometimes at the plant, but usually at our home where they would share a meal and talk war and their futures. We still have photos of some in our possession.

One of these men lived in Sellersville and was really a great guy in every way. He fell in love with a lovely girl also living in the area. He wanted in the worst way to get a date with her but didn't have the confidence to do so, not even how to approach her. He asked Dad for advice, and Dad gave him the confidence and assured him that he was her equal, and she would date him.

Dad found out she was an outstanding roller skater and could be found at the rink at Menlo Park in Perkasie. So the plan was to go there and start a conversation since he could also skate. The plan worked perfectly, and they were married either before the war ended or right after. I know he also took Dad's advice and joined the navy. They had a wonderful life together and raised a family. Dad shared this story with me maybe the year they were married, so I enjoyed the relationship that I was in on even as a young boy. Their names were Bill and Veronica Rothensberger.

The fabric used to protect the steel workers was asbestos. It is illegal to use this fabric in America today because of the effects it has on the lungs to develop mesothelioma and lung cancer. In the early days, it was unknown, and no one knew the danger since it usually took many years for this to develop. Dad told the story later in life, when the results were being told about asbestos, how two medical doctors were involved in the company, Green Tweed, that developed the asbestos cloth.

I remember Dad taking me to the factory on a Saturday morning, and I'm sure it was before the war because only a few people were there. We went into a larger room that was called the carding room where they used a pitch fork and shoveled the raw asbestos, which in its rawest form is a very splintered rock. They took these fibers and pitched them into a machine that eventually spun them into your yarn and then woven into cloth.

The point of this explanation is the air that morning in the room was like a fine snowstorm. They had single light bulbs in sockets hanging from the ceiling, which only dramatized more the snow sight I saw that morning.

Mr. Shive was the man working in the carding room and lived on Washington Avenue in Sellersville. He actually lived to be an old man, despite the terrible environment he worked in. He had a billy goat with a cart that we took rides in several times as children. Up and down the alley was the road he took us on.

The war changed our lives because it became the central focus in all of our lives. It changed the way we ate, dressed, traveled, thought, and had God back in peoples' lives. From the common man to the president, Franklin Roosevelt, God was looked to for the victory.

No longer could you go into a store and purchase anything you desired. You were given food stamps and meat stamps every month, and you had to stick to them—no exceptions. Mom and Dad would figure every week how many items they could buy.

The government encouraged victory gardens, and Dad, with other neighbors, had them in the fields above Hughes Avenue, just behind Ziggy Shelly's plumbing garages. They would hire a black man with a horse to plow and disc it in the spring, and us kids would always be there for the great occasion. They were fairly large gardens, about twelve yards by twenty yards each. We grew corn, tomatoes, potatoes, cabbage, lettuce, peppers, red beets, and beans.

Mother canned the tomatoes and string beans along with peaches that were bought at an orchard in Spinnerstown. This was a lot of work after both working hard all day. It's amazing what you can accomplish with no TV. Paul and I had a small garden next to Dad's where we grew a few vegetables and helped or hindered in his garden.

Gasoline was also rationed, and you were given a special sticker on the front window with, I believe, a stamp book also. The stickers were lettered A, B, C, D, E, F, about three inches tall. Depending on your drive to work and the type of work you did gave you the amount of gas you could purchase each month, and the lettered stamp would show this.

Dad had a good stamp because of his critical work and the distance to North Wales and back. There was very little gas for a vacation or visiting many relatives and friends because you still had shopping and other essential things to take care of.

If someone needed gas to do a vacation, the men on Hughes Avenue would siphon gas with a rubber hose from one car to another by sucking the air out of the hose with the hose in your mouth. This was risky and dangerous to do, but they did. I saw it done many times in our own alley.

I don't remember rationing stamps for clothing, but there was not an overabundance of anything. Mother was always hand sewing patches on clothing, especially mending our socks. As I mentioned before, Dad repaired our shoes and the one family whose father was in the marines. There were a lot of hand-me-downs and sharing among relatives and friends to keep everyone clothed.

I mentioned before about having no metal toys at all for about two years, and this included bikes, express wagons, ice skates, etc. But as always, you would hear of people buying from the black market certain items that were purchased illegally. Sometimes these items could come from stores that had excess inventories stored away and now could sell at a good profit. Items like sugar, chocolates, rubber, and silk stockings were very scarce.

The Willow Grove Naval Airbase, which was only about eighteen miles away, was very busy as you can imagine and was another reminder to us children that we were really fighting a war. They trained and flew over Sellersville regularly. They came in fighting formations of four to six planes in a group and usually flew fairly low because you could often see the pilots flying these fighters. The roar of the propeller-driven planes was loud and exhilarating to us as we stopped whatever we were doing to watch this show of awesome power.

Comic books were big, big entertainment during all the 1940s and especially during the war because most of our heroes were now fighting the Japs and Germans and winning every battle. These picture booklets with word captions were really entertaining, and we all had our favorites when buying these booklets. Trading books took place with almost every edition. Without television, this was a good replacement to keep us occupied and our imaginations working overtime.

The Second World War did impact our lives, and I had the privilege to experience it from the eyes and ears of a young boy and would never change this time in my life for anything. The evening the war was declared over I will never forget. Every neighbor came out of their homes and started shouting, "the war is over!" You have to remember like most communities our people were friendly, but reserved emotionally, so it was a sight just to see your parents with their neighbor friends congratulating each other. People then got in their cars and drove all other town blowing their horns and hollering out their windows.

The fire trucks came out, and they also rang their bells and sirens on the trucks going through the streets. When they came up Hughes Avenue, us kids were out running around, and we all decided to jump on the fire trucks, and so we did. We rode the trucks over to the firehouse and then got off when we saw the big iron ring with its big hammer used in the early days of the borough to sound the fire alarm.

We rang this loud noisemaker till we couldn't move the heavy hammer anymore. We returned home and went into our 122 Hughes Avenue and listened with our parents to the details of victory on the radio that ended this epic time in our young lives.

After the war, Sellersville was chosen as a new site for a Pennsylvania National Guard unit. It was 1948 when a new building was erected along the park system. Thirty-Second Quartermaster Group is housed there. Many of the returning servicemen joined, I believe, partly because of the camaraderie they enjoyed. They have been activated several times, including the Iraq War. There was tremendous pride when we saw these heroes march in those early days in the Memorial Day Parades.

I must mention we lost our baseball field when they erected their building, but it was okay because we still had the Macadam Street of Hughes Avenue to skin our knees on.

10

Lake Lenape

Summer time at Lake Lenape where we would swim.

Lake Lenape, better known to us kids as the creek, was very important to me while growing up on Hughes Avenue. We spent a lot of time fishing. I never had a real fishing pole with a reel. All of us kids only had a long stick with a fishing line, hook, sinker, and floater. We used mainly earthworms and crayfish tails that looked like shrimp for fish bait. We fished mainly below the waterfalls and caught sunfish. It was fun just to catch them, and no one ever ate them.

Lake Lenape Park in early Spring.

One of the strangest happenings in my life was one day two teenage brothers from another part of town, for whatever reason, challenged each other to swallow whole live minnow fish. There were plenty of minnows below the falls, and they had a net to catch them. They probably swallowed at least a dozen each until both gave up the

Fishing below the dam at Lake Lenape.
Yes that me with the fishing pole.

challenge. It made me sick just to watch this stupid challenge.

The creek at the scout cabin was where we did our swimming. It was about four feet deep there, so we could easily stand. Across from the cabin, on the opposite side of the creek, was a cement pier that you could shallow dive off of, but we very seldom did. We just had a good time swimming and playing swim tag. During a dry spell in summer, the water would barely go over the falls; then green algae would collect and completely cover the water. That didn't bother us. We would swim any way and simply push the algae away. It's a wonder we didn't get sick. Maybe we did and never figured it out.

Also, on the cabin side was a large tree that the Sea Scouts hung a thick rope on to allow you to swing out over the water and then jump in. Fun, fun, fun!

The Sea Scouts owned the cabin and was made up of boys sixteen years old and older. They had about six or eight canoes that were locked down outside the cabin. Once you gain their friendship and confidence, they would let you use them, which we really enjoyed, but there was no goofing off like sinking a canoe, or it would take a very long time to use them again.

Fritz Kemmerer was the well-known skipper of this group and was highly regarded in Sea Scouting in America. He was also the last survivor of the Last Man's Club of the First World War in the community. He lived into his nineties, which was old when he died.

Scout Cabin in Lake Lenape Park

People at this time had their private canoes chained to trees along the creek, and no one disturbed them. Can you imagine today leaving your canvas-covered canoe overnight with not even the police watching over them?

Jack Bedford and I were at the Main Street Bridge that spanned the creek on the day they tore down the old cement bridge. I was only about four or five years old because the brass plate with the date of 1940 is on the new bridge and is still there today. We climbed on the cement guardrail and watched as they dropped a huge iron ball chained to a hoist. This is how they destroyed the old bridge. Every time they dropped the ball, it shook the bridge that we had to really hang on because the drop on the creek side was about twenty feet down. After about fifteen minutes, we were chased off and for our own good.

When they started the demolition of the bridge, they laid huge slabs about three feet by five feet and about eight inches to ten inches thick across the shallow water, maybe about forty feet from the bridge on the falls side. I'm sure they could be found today by very little uncovering. The reason for the path from one side to the other was for people to walk back and forth in town. This was the only way anyone could walk to get to school or shopping if you didn't own a car, and many people still didn't own one. Cars had to travel to Perkasie to reach each end of the community. I don't know for sure, but it seemed like it took a year.

Brickyard road was a common name for Park Avenue because just beyond the armory is where they dug into the earth to remove the good clay to make bricks. At that time, about 1890 and into the 1920s, they fired the bricks there also. Sellersville's biggest building boom happened at the same time; therefore, most of the homes in that time period came from Brickyard Road. Up to about 1980, you could still see two huge pits about eight feet deep, twenty yards by forty yards each, in the ground. Today they are filled, and condos or row homes are built over them.

Another interesting aspect of this business is that it was run by Dad's uncles or great-uncles. They were Clymers, nevertheless.

The Sellersville Fireman's Carnival was also held along the parkway on Park Avenue next to the armory. The carnival was there during the war years and probably a good number of years before. I always loved the carnival, and this was my first taste of it. Parking was never a problem because there was only street parking, but most people walked. The main attraction was always the cowboy Western shows, which were the only entertainment available and what the people wanted. The carnivals were heavily attended because it was a great family and community outing.

After the war, the carnival was moved to its current location behind the firehouse because a larger area was needed to accommodate larger crowds with better parking and conveniences afforded at the firehouse. This was without a doubt the highlight of the summer season. It ran for three consecutive weekends in July and August, Fridays and Saturdays only. The shows remained country Western, and they always had the best groups available. The shows were always free and always brought out the people. We were given as children fifty cents each for every evening, which was a good amount of money because you could buy a hamburger for fifteen cents and hot dogs, sodas, and ice cream for ten cents each.

We would try to win prizes at the game wheels for five or ten cents a spin. The firemen would let us play these game wheels, even the money wheels at five cents a spin. Our favorite was called the Big Six. It had three numbers in each row, so you had a pretty good chance at winning. The wheel was about six feet in diameter, and yes, we did win, and we did lose. The local fire company controlled the games, food, and everything. There was no outside companies involved in the carnival. We always tried our skill at the penny pitch and tossing small wooden rings around a fancy-painted cane or a Hawaiian lieu to wear around your neck to show off that night. Humble kids we were.

We would be on the ground as soon as the carnival opened. Usually our parents would come with the younger brothers around 8:30 PM to catch the show at 9:00 PM. We would find them to beg for more money.

"Could we just have ten cents more for a hot dog?"

"We're still hungry."

I know you also understand this game; you played it also. If any organization is a representation of our community, it is our fire company. They gave so much to our community. We will always be indebted to them. They were and are a blessing to us.

Several times while living on Hughes Avenue, a small circus would come to town. This was really a big deal for all of us because of the excitement of seeing elephants, horses, and watching the workers erect the large tent using the elephants to pull it up. I think as kids, we got more entertainment watching all this activity at a distance, before we even went into the show the next day.

We thought the show was exciting because we saw very little live entertainment growing up. My, how television again changed so many things. The tents were at first set up along Park Avenue, just west of the National Guard Armory, which was not yet built. It was then moved to the parking lot behind the firehouse because a larger area was needed.

In autumn, we headed for the creek to gather nuts because there were many nut trees, but only three different types: a small hickory nut, a black English walnut that was very tasty but difficult to get to because it had an outside covering over the nut that stained your fingers and then a very hard shell, and the other was some kind of oak nut that we never ate, but simply liked the smooth-colored shape.

We would take a hammer or just whack them with a rock against a rock. We felt like we were pioneers or living like the early settlers living off the land. It was the feeling of the cool air and colored autumn leaves and smell in the air that made this another special time in my life.

Winter in Lake Lenape was another interesting period of living on Hughes Avenue. The creek froze over around the Christmas holidays, and it seemed to stay that way the whole winter. We would play on the ice a lot during the winter. The kids my age while we lived there never took to ice skating. I'm not sure why; maybe we didn't have money for ice skates, and during the war, skates were hard to come by, but we were there with our sleds, and we would push each other up and down the creek from the falls up to Perkasie at the twin bridges and back again. It was enjoyable to watch adults, especially young adults, skate and race on the creek.

We were usually on the ice in the evenings when we were free and would beg our parents to let us go there. Some people would turn on their car lights to enable people to skate, but the real fun of the evening was to be around the bonfires made to keep warm and help with the lighting. It always felt so good to get close to the fire, and to help maintain in keeping the fire fed with wood, we would continue to gather from the fallen branches.

Today the creek hardly freezes over, not so in the days of my youth. Maybe the water is moving too fast because of the changes to keep the flow moving for the nuclear plant in Limerick? The creek would break up in early Spring and overflow on the grounds bordering the creek. This was quite a sight to see in itself because the ice was thick, and the pieces were huge in size.

*Ice that broke up every spring at Lake Lenape with Scout
Cabin in background and my niece Megan Clymer,
Barry and Pam's daughter, in foreground.*

Dad often told me about the ice house that was once located
about forty yards from Wilmer Myer's garage toward Perkasie and
on his side of the creek. They would cut ice during the winter and
store it in a large barn-type building only constructed of wood, no
insulation. They didn't have insulation as we know it today, but they
layered the ice with sawdust, and this would keep it long into the
summer. Can't imagine the work this must have been and in the cold
conditions.

Dad also related the story of a drowning under the ice at the
creek when he was a boy. I believe one of his brothers, Uncle Irvin
or Wilson, who died at fourteen years of age at Quarry was there
that day. It was a foolish game boys played called pickle when they
either cut a hole in the ice or found an area that wasn't frozen very
hard and would take turns jumping over it. As you can guess, one
of the boys didn't make it and slipped under the ice and could not
find the hole. Some of the boys jumped into the freezing water

with sticks in hand trying to locate him but to no avail. They never played that game again, and I'm sure it was a life changer in their young lives.

Flooding at Lake Lenape seemed to happen almost every year, but only one time a year when it happened. It wasn't until the 1960s or 1970s that the state stepped in and widened the creek on the firehouse side of the bridge. Before that, there was only a narrow gorge for the water to pass through, and a flood could easily occur. The water would back up so bad that all the yards on Hughes Avenue would be covered with a foot of water, as well as the street itself. I have pictures to actually show this.

On the other side of town, up to Walnut Street, would be flooded. Fritz's Drugstore, next to the trolley station, would have to give away their ice cream because of the water.

Flood water from Lke Lenape in our back yard. Hughes Ave.

Fritzs' store and Lehigh Valley trolley station on Main street during a flood. (Courtesy of Sellersville Museum)

As kids, we would wait till the water subsided enough so our parents would allow us to go out into the streets and play in the gutters, since the streets itself had a fairly high crown and deep gutters on both sides of the street. They were brick lined and fairly smooth. The water would be rushing very hard yet from the fields, so it was the powerful force of water that we enjoyed. Resisting that was so much fun. There was about eighteen inches in height of water gushing down both sides of the street.

11

Dad Finds His Vocation

Dad's uncle, William Scheetz, known as Uncle Will, was the father figure to our Dad since Dad's father died when he was eight. Uncle Will was Dad's mother's brother. He owned the Old Mill along the park that fronts on Main Street at the Main Street Bridge. He sold all kinds of used parts, tools, and other collectibles, and cars sold as scrap metal. The mill water race was a separate stream from the main creek that flowed near the mill to turn the water wheel. They had to block off the entrance of the water but now decided to fill in the rest of the stream.

Uncle Will hired Dad to do this during the Great Depression at one dollar a day. There was no work available, so Dad was hired to fill it in with scrap cars and dirt. As a boy going to the falls to fish, we would walk over those cars that were being exposed by water erosion. Over the years I never knew this story until years later as a young adult.

Dad also did some truck driving during Prohibition. He would take a stake body truck and haul potatoes from an area outside of Bethlehem toward the Pocono Mountains and deliver them to Philadelphia and Atlantic City. Inside of certain potato sacks were marked bags that contained moonshine, i.e., illegal whisky to be dropped off. He said he never knew the sacks with bottles but knew he was delivering this illegal merchandise.

Uncle Will's name was constantly part of Dad's conversation when talking about his life growing up and as a young man. He lived on Green Street across from 27 Green Street where we lived after moving from Hughes Avenue. He died about 1938 and is buried in Sellersville, next to the equipment shed. I never knew him, of course, but Mother said that on my birth, he gave me a child's metal bowl with utensils that she kept for a long time.

Dad modeling an asbestos pair of pants used for fire rescue

The other major part he played in Dad's life was getting him a job at Green Tweed in North Wales. Uncle Will had been working there for some time, and they put out the word they were looking for someone that had sewing experience to help develop a department to manufacture gloves and clothing for the steel industry using asbestos cloth that they were first to perfect.

Dad had very limited experience in sewing since he was working at Lutz's pants factory where Mother also worked. His job was using a bar tacker, which required little sewing skill, but knowing Dad, he probably did some sewing on a single needle machine, but he was limited in the skill.

It goes back to the old story that it's not what you know but who you know. Dad applied for the job and got it. Uncle Will, I'm absolutely certain, had to pull some strings for this to happen. Judging from the other members of Uncle Will's family whom I did get to know, I think I know a little about his personality. He was an intelligent person who had his own business at the Old Mill. He was a persuasive talker with a sense of humor, a large body frame, and a stocky build. This gave Dad and eventually our family a good living and us children security and a good life.

Dad would always drive Uncle Will to work with him for as long as he lived, and I believe some others from town as well every day.

Dad stayed with Green Tweed until a few years after war when they decided to move his department to Glenside, just outside of Philadelphia. This did not sit too well with him. He took the train back and forth every day, which became a chore. He even thought about being a conductor at one point. But he met a salesman on the train that sold ladies' apparel and lived just outside of the Clymer homestead where Dad's grandparents once lived on Clymer Avenue. His name was Bert Hibler, and they started a safety-clothing business called Lenape Safety Clothing. This lasted for about two to three years and was located in Perkasie on the second floor at Ninth and Market Streets across from the Perkasie Cemetery.

Dad was also a prankster in his younger days at work. This was typical in the workplace. I don't think it's practiced very much anymore. I personally never liked it, and when I had any authority or my own business, I tried to put an end to it because all it did was to make someone angry or hurt.

I remember a few stories he told me. They would take Limburger cheese and spread it on someone's car engine. If they didn't smell it when they got into their car, they sure did when the engine warmed up, and it would take days for it to disappear, even after cleaning it off the engine.

When Dad was taking the train to Glenside, one day the train was held up for a long time at a stop, and a worker for Dad, Irwin "Poppy" Fretz, was also taking the train every day. Poppy Fretz wanted to see why the train was being held up and stuck his head out the window. For fun, Dad closed the window to one of the position stops and couldn't get it to release once the train started moving. No matter what he tried, he called for the conductor to help but to no avail. Finally, they had to pull the emergency stop cord to stop the train, and somehow did get the window open.

There was a worker that was giving a lot of people grief. So Dad and some workers figured it was payback time and somehow disguised chocolate Ex-Lax as a Hershey bar and offered it to him. He took the bait, and, as they say, the rest is history.

In another episode, Dad just hired a new man. First day on the job he was told to keep an eye on a certain worker because he's been having troubles in his life and had made statements about taking his life, even by jumping out the three-story windows on the floor where they now both worked. This story, of course, was completely fabricated, and what the new man didn't know was outside the window was a rather narrow roof, about four feet below the window.

Well, the worker that was supposed to be sick was sure the new guy was watching, raced to the open window, shouting, "I'm going to do it." And he jumped.

Of course, the poor new guy was shouting, "Don't do it!" And also raced over to stop him.

After the first man jumped, he landed safely, turned looking up smiling, and said, "Hello, are you okay?"

Dad was loved and respected by all his workers. He had a good sense of humor, including dry humor. He was just a good person to be around. But he was a good worker, and people worked hard for him. He was a good conversationalist but didn't waste time standing around talking and killing time. He understood how important time was in production.

Dad was actually a pioneer in the manufacturing of asbestos gloves and clothing. He was hired with limited knowledge in sewing, but he was determined to make good on this one-time opportunity. He designed hand protection in gloves and mitts and clothing of coats, hoods, leggings, blankets, and everything involved with this new product.

He set the piece rates, fixed many of the sewing machines as they needed repair, met the quality and production standards set at Green Tweed that when he left the plant in Glenside, they closed it completely. One of the top men in management there, William Jordan, decided to sell the products once sold at Green Tweed and had Dad make them for him. They supplied all the Bethlehem Steel plants, which numbered about five and was the backbone for many years.

No one could figure out how to use the heavy yarn of asbestos as a sewing thread to sew blankets and other thick layers of asbestos where high temperatures were needed to protect in sewing these items. Heavy cotton thread was the only thing available at this time. Dad figured out how to do this and was the first one to make it work. He needed to lubricate the yarn because asbestos was on the fragile side. It was a mineral from a fibrous rock found only in Canada. By using the clothing washing soap Ivory Snow, he had the perfect lubricant after mixing it with water. None of us children ever got involved with the business until after we moved from Hughes Avenue.

Throwing quoits and horseshoes was very popular in the '30s and '40s, and Dad excelled in quoits. He pitched quoits in North Wales on his lunch hour, and they did have an hour in those days, so he became quite good. On Hughes Avenue, the men would pitch them at the side of Danny Mullin's yard since he had an end house at the far side of the row houses. They dug clay from Lake Lenape, probably where the brickyard was located, and they were set to go. In the evenings, when it was convenient, four men would be pitching quoits, and we would be watching them. That's how I knew he was good.

12

Personalities

The Sellersville playground, known as B. Earl Druckenmiller Playground today, occupied an important place in my life, and most children in the community because of one man, B. Earl Druckenmiller, known affectionately as Drucky. He was one of the most outstanding personalities Sellersville ever had. Born in town, he taught in the high school physical education, and he coached all four major sports: football, basketball, baseball, and track at the same time—and mostly without any assistants.

He had championships galore and always had contending teams. He coached at Sellersville High School and Sell-Perk High School and finished at Pennridge High School. He developed his track teams during gym classes and had state champions in relays with records that stood for years. He himself starred in track at Muhlenberg College.

My mother would eat her lunches with Drucky's mother in her house across from the pants factory, which is torn down now. She and Mrs. Druckenmiller became friends as both worked together.

Drucky was involved in the community activities, service clubs, Boy Scouts. He taught in Sunday School at St. Michael's and anywhere he was called upon for help. I could write a book on him just from the limited knowledge I have.

Earl Drunckenmiller with "Lindy" and "Billy," two long-time favorite playground ponies.

He would never be out of a conversation and could talk on any subject. He impacted all our lives because he was a very moral person and could not stand kids that never showed respect to adults, parents, and teachers. He would go after them, and they knew it. Yet he loved to have fun and a good sense of humor. He had a heart of gold and would help kids who couldn't afford baseball gloves and other sporting equipment. He went to Philadelphia about every week to Mitchell & Ness, a well-known sporting goods store where he would work deals and buy goods for everyone in town at great prices. People contacted him all the time, and his house was a busy place, but he always had time, and he always looked in great shape. He lived to be about ninety-five years old.

Drucky maintained the playground all by himself, mowed all the grass, maintained three clay tennis courts, the baseball diamonds, supervised the summer children activities. He had one or two ponies that he owned and kept at the playground.

He had a pony buggy that he would give you rides if you picked a certain amount of tussled weeds that his riding mower would not cut. We would all be out picking, usually hundreds at a time, to get our rides, but no one ever counted them.

He loved to have special days during summer like a watermelon cut when he would bring in an all black children's camp of boys to play baseball against us, and then everyone celebrated with the watermelons.

We loved the days we would gather on the pavilion that no longer exists, but he would have us answer questions on things concerning sports or mind challenges, like "Raise your hand when you think a minute is up."

"How tall is our flagpole here at the grounds?"

It was the great prizes he gave out: Sell-Perk sweatshirts, T-shirts, baseballs, hats, athletic socks, and even a basketball or football for a grand price. You can see how he would win you over, and yet there was a certain amount of fearful respect for him.

The wading pool was our main attraction when we walked from Hughes Avenue to the playground. It was circular, about twenty feet in diameter with a sprinkling fountain in the center that filled and fed water into the pool. At the center, the depth was only about three feet deep. But we had a great time playing in it and then playing on the playground equipment and going for the pony rides.

Years later, I had often thought about the impact Drucky had on the community and, especially, the playground, so I called my friend Dick Coll, who was borough manager at the time and suggested to name the playground after Drucky while he was living to show our appreciation. Dick said he also had the same thoughts, and I believe I had a small part in honoring Drucky by the community he served so well.

Kiwanis installed wading pool on playground.

Frederick's Barbershop at Temple Avenue in the Odd Fellows Building, Main and Temple Avenue, was the watering hole in the community where men gathered every day to talk about everything in the community: sports world, the world, politics, and you name it. We went there for our haircuts after Arto died, who took us to Mr. Clemmer on Clymer Avenue.

I would sit and listen to all this talk, since you had no appointment times. Lee Wilhelm; Pastor Fred Billmeyer; Bob Bergey, a car dealer; Jim Hackett, a sports writer and community leader; and faces I remember but names fail me. A lot of businessmen would come in for shaves every day, so Charlie and Lloyd, who were brothers and owned the business that eventually Charlie alone owned, built up a daily clientele, and so the conversation would continue.

One day, Eddie Moyer was waiting for his turn for a haircut. A boy about eight or nine years old was flipping a quarter in the air and

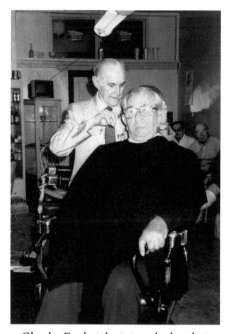

catching it in his mouth when the quarter got stuck in his throat and could not breathe. He turned beet red, and Charlie turned around and saw him. Charlie hit him on the back, but to no avail, so he picked him up by his ankles, turned him upside down and shook him until the quarter came out like a slot machine.

Another part of my life that took place in the Odd Fellows Building was playing bingo on Friday evenings and run by the Lodge. My brother Paul and I went regularly for almost two years. We never won that much because we could only afford one card each.

Charles Frederick giving the last hair cut to Fritz Kemmerer, last survivor of World War I and well known in the community especiall for the work in Sea scouting locally and in the United States

Jim Shelly, a friend of ours from Hughes Avenue, and his grandmother took us with them, and we enjoyed the evening and continued to go back. They sold coffee, soda, hot dogs, etc., during the evening, which made it interesting for us. I believe we were the only children there.

It is interesting how safe the community was in those days with only Mike Hallman, the only policeman who depended on his wife to drive their car as a police car. Yet the town was safe because of the strong families that taught right and wrong and children that obeyed them.

After the bingo games were over, we would walk home by ourselves at eleven at night. We were only ten, eleven, or twelve years old. The streets were deserted except for a hot dog- hamburger truck that parked along Main Street across from the Washington House Hotel to sell to people leaving the Lodge at the games. We never felt fear or threatened all the way home.

Menlo Park in Perkasie was a special place for our family on Sunday afternoons. We spent many afternoons there. We would arrive about 4:00 PM to watch the free outdoor country Western show that changed every week. They had a nice stage with park benches that seated about five hundred or more people. We would enjoy the show and then go for a carousel ride, the same one that Perkasie saved and is still used on special days during the summer. The park was still well-attended even though they had limited rides for the people. We would be allowed to ride the Whip, the bumping cars only about half the times we visited the park.

Menlo Park Carousel that we rode every time we visited the park in Perkasie.

The carousel we rode every visit and sometimes two or three times. There were three or four rides for small children. A large swimming pool took the place of a community pool. Bowling alleys and roller skating rink rounded out the amusements.

Family picnics and social picnics were still a big attraction to bring people into the park because they could use about half-dozen pavilions among the many shade trees. Many years the Scheetz family reunions were held there. This would be relatives from Dad's mother's side of the family. These were happy times as we looked forward going to the Menlo Park on these warm, sunny afternoons with, again, no TV to keep us home watching sports that would soon change all our lives.

We had heard about the television for some years before I actually saw it. On our upright floor model radio, there was actually a push button marked TV. We just assumed one day a screen would be adapted into the radio.

The first time I watched television was around 1947 or 1948. Earl Moyer owned and operated an electric store that sold radios, washing machines, refrigerators, etc. The store was located at Main and Walnut Streets where the little town park is located. This is where the former Hildebidle building was located.

We were walking home from the Sellersville playground on a Saturday afternoon, and as we walked past the showroom window, we saw a television set in black and white with a fuzzy picture, but we could see it was a Phillies baseball game. We came into the store with other people and watched the game for maybe twenty minutes because we knew, as kids, we were taking up space for adults, but it was my first time to see something of future impact on all of us.

As kids, if we wanted to see television, we would walk over to Moyer's store and see if a set was turned on. There were very few sets sold the first year or two, but on Hughes Avenue, Warren Huff purchased one for his family. Now we had a place to watch television, but there were very, very few programs telecast. The screen was only about eight inches. Yes, very small and a lot of snow, and the picture would roll over. Someone had to be almost always standing at the set to keep adjusting it. You had to pull the shades at the windows to keep it dark during the day. The antenna was fastened to the roof using a wooden pole, which broke several times from wind and storms and had to be replaced.

It was quite an experience with those early sets. The shows that we watched on Huff's television were very old western reruns that were made back in the early thirties. There were only three channels, and long periods during the day there were no shows, only test patterns for hours on end.

Our family never got a television until almost 1950 when we moved to Green Street. Dad just couldn't see buying a set with all the problems I just listed above. By 1950, the sets were much larger, the picture problems greatly improved, but only four channels were available. The first week we sat on the floor and watched the test patterns waiting for a program to appear. Once the programs like Milton Berle's, *Ed Sullivan Show, Howdy Doody*, and some other key shows were launched did television take off with major league sports thrown into the mix.

Television changed our lifestyle once the programs caught on. People changed their social meetings in the evenings so they could watch their favorite shows. We, as Boy Scouts, changed our Tuesday meeting time to Mondays because Milton Berle was on that night. People stayed home Saturday night to watch *The Jackie Gleason Show* and Sid Caesar's *Your Show of Shows*, and *The Ed Sullivan Show* Sunday nights with sports Saturday and Sunday afternoons. They were all clean fun with great comedy. It was comedy through Milton Berle that sold more television sets to the American people than any other person, show or reason.

13

Scouting

Franklin, Boy Scout at Valley Forge Jamboree 1950

oy Scouting for me began as a young boy, maybe nine years old in Cub Scouting. We met in a home on Grandview Avenue in Sellersville with our leader, Naomi Cressmen. Brother Paul and I both had the dark-blue uniforms with the neck scarves and hats. We were eager to be there every week and did our memory work and especially looked forward to the craft part of the night with always a special treat before we went home. One of the crafts we worked on was making leather compass pocket holders that we could put our direction compass into and be worn over our belt.

Somehow our dad got involved in this project and supplied soft, smooth skin tan leather that could have been deerskins. They were large pieces of leftover scrap from his work but plenty large enough to cut out these pockets. We had to use a handheld punch, the kind with a rotating head to make holes all around the leather and then lacing these holes, top and bottom, with strips cut from leather into laces. They turned out to be very attractive, but some of the young boys needed adult help to hand punch the holes, and Dad even helped one evening to compete the project.

William Hill and Roy Rodgers with trigger at the Hill Farm.

While I was still in Cub Scouting about 1946, Roy Rogers and his famous horse Trigger were in town and staying at the well-known Hills Palomino Horse Farm at the edge of our community. Most people knew this happened every year but no one knew exactly why. This particular year, our Cub Scout troop along with other Scouting units in the vicinity were invited out to the Hills Farm on a Saturday afternoon to see the "King of the Cowboys" and his horse Trigger. I was not able to attend because I had no transportation that day. But I did see a home movie of Roy doing a show for all the Scouts that day. Mr. Hills son, Bill Jr., was also a part of the Cub Pack, so all got to see the film.

I believe it's worth noting how big a star both were at the time and the connection with the farm. Did Trigger come from any of the 20 Palomino horses quartered there? The answer is no family tree for Trigger at the farm. Trigger came from a stable in San Diego, California at a cost of 2,500 dollars, which was a lot of money for that time. But there is a chance that one of the Hills horses was used as a double for Trigger because of the strenuous schedule for this horse. Roy did buy a horse from the farm but he could never tell his audience of children and adults that they were watching a double do the tricks that only Trigger could do. Trigger died in 1965 at 33 years old.

They starred in 88 movies and 100 television episodes and innumerable rodeos and personal appearances. It was while Roy would do a rodeo in Philadelphia every year that he needed a home for Trigger before performing his next show at Madison Square Garden. It was then that he was introduced to William Hill Sr. and they became very good friends and the arrangements were made for Trigger.

Roy Rogers was a great entertainer. He was a Rhinestone Cowboy that could sing, do tricks with his horse, relate very well with an audience, good looking and could always get the bad guys in the movies. When I was a young boy at this time, Dale Evans was not part of his life yet. But most important, he was a wonderful Christian man with his wife Dale. He would always give a testimony to Christ as his Savior and had a definite impact on the young lives watching and listening to his every move. Roy, how we could use you now. He was part of the "Greatest Generation."

After Cub Scouting, we went onto Boy Scouting. I was about twelve years old and enjoyed every year I was a scout. We met on the first floor, ground level of the old Sellersville High School building, which is now the borough building on the alley side of the building.

Harold Milligan was our scoutmaster, and we really enjoyed his leadership. He enjoyed the experience as much as we did. He never pushed us hard to complete all our merit badges to become Eagle scouts, but he did encourage us, and I did have a small amount I possessed.

What he did for us was to enjoy scouting itself by camping out in the different woods, going to scout camp for a week every year, taking overnight hikes and having an organized but fun time at our meeting every Tuesday nights.

Our favorite place to camp at was on the hill side of Cathill Road facing the 309 bypass on Bill Bates's farm property. Bill was also a scout.

One evening there were only three of us sleeping over with our pup tents. We would always cook our own meals on an open fire with only a circle of rocks to contain the fires. We really enjoyed roughing it.

This one night, about one or two in the morning, Ken Huff and I were awakened by the third boy saying he wanted to go home because he was scared by some noise he heard. It could have been someone in the woods. He already had all his clothes on but was afraid to walk up to Cathill Road by himself and wanted us to get him up to it. Ken and I only had our underwear on because we would return to camp. When we got to the road, it was really dark, and he asked us to just go a little further with him. Well, pretty soon, we got scared and thought he might be right and decided we're not going back but going home also.

Our only problem was we only had our white underwear on. We had to sneak into town, avoiding any cars and especially a police, which we actually saw and lay down behind the railroad tracks where the old footbridge stood at Church Street. We made it home; our doors were never locked. We were now living on Green Street, and each made it to our beds. We told our parents the next morning, got on other clothes, and went back to retrieve our other clothes and camping gear. No other scout ever found out about this episode.

I believe the highest rank I achieved was first-class scout. The highest achievement was order of the arrow, and in my last year in scouting I no longer can remember the title, but it gave you top authority in the troop next to the scoutmaster, something like a sergeant in the army.

Sellersville had a respected position in scouting since it was troop number 1, the first organized troop in Bucks County. Our father, as a boy, was part of this program, and we still have his uniform in the family. Brother Paul actually donated my uniform to the Sellersville Museum, at least that's what he told me, and politicians do not lie.

Just a funny story about Dad in Scouts. He told me he was sixteen years old and had his own car. The scouts were helping with the Grand View Hospital Fete, which was a big community event to raise money on the grounds of the hospital for support. Dad was picking up cakes in the community for the cake sale. He would put them on the front seat and in the trunk since it only sat two people.

Days later, someone asked him if he ever picked up a certain lady's most famous cake since no one knew anything about it. Dad looked in the trunk, and, sure enough, there it was. He never told anyone about it. Maybe he took it home and ate it; I don't remember the ending.

Talking about cake sales, the troop had one for me to send me to the national jamboree in Valley Forge in 1950. This was the largest ever held in the history of scouting. More than fifty thousand scouts from all over the world were there.

President Truman and General Eisenhower were the speakers on two evenings that week. It was a time I will never forget. We spent ten days there, slept in pup tents, had to cook our own food, and were divided by states and the counties. Bucks County had about thirty to forty boys there.

We all had work to do, usually with the cooking and eating, but were on the go all day. The thing I and all scouts enjoyed was trading with other states and countries. I traded for neckerchief slides from all over the world, especially the States. I had a great collection and would win a blue ribbon every year at the Sell-Perk Farm Show.

Before we left for the jamboree, the county supplied us with items to use for trade like neckerchief slides, monogram county badges, and community companies gave me and Dave Weidemoyer, another scout that paid his own way, products from their companies to use for trade. I also made things to take for trade and a good thing happened when Dad and his business partner bought the ship model factory building with all its contents of wooden ship models in kits. I got to take dozens of these models and traded like crazy. Pretty soon I was selling them for money.

Bill Brickajlik was a scout from Silverdale, later the owner of the business on 309 in Quakertown that bears his name. Bill saw the success I was having and, even at his early age, saw how to make a buck. He said he would help me sell them. I agreed I would continue to get my price, and anything above he could get was his. Maybe I launched his career.

I called Dad and asked him to bring as much as possible when he and Mother and the rest of the family planned to come visit me. He had his trunk loaded with them, and we sold and traded them all. The traffic was bumper to bumper. I don't know how they ever found me.

I spent three summers at scout camp near Point Pleasant, Bucks County, called Camp Ockanickon. It was a great time of camp life with competition against about six to eight other scout troops from Bucks County. The camp setting was in a mountainous area that was wooded where we slept four boys to an army-style tent with a wooden floor. The pool, administration building, and mess hall were in a clearing where games could also be played. They had a full-time doctor and nurse on staff and a black cook who worked at the University of Pennsylvania during the school sessions.

The mess hall was a place we all looked forward to, except when we had KP duty, which consisted of peeling potatoes using a machine that sanded off the skins and coloring margarine that was in one-pound plastic bags that had a small amount of orange dye in them. You had to squeeze them with your hands forever until the dye made it look yellow like butter.

Before the meals, we sang our scouting songs and other fun songs, which unified us as Boy Scouts. The food was always good, and we had plenty. Just in case you needed more, the snack shop was open where ice cream, candy, T-shirts, etc., were sold. Somehow I was always there with my friends.

I became a Boy Scout about 1948-1949. This was only a few years after the Second World War, and in all the cities, there were stores called Army Navy Stores that sold everything you could imagine, like canteens, life rafts, tents, backpacks, shovels, picks, flashlights, buckets, clothing, and thousands of other items. The stores were jammed, and the prices were very low. This was perfect for scouting, and Dad and I were with the first scoutmaster (he left after about six months) when we went to Philly to buy for our troop.

I went with them because of Dad, and I enjoyed it immensely, buying a canteen and some other things for myself. The first scoutmaster's name was Walter Kenesiky.

Another interesting story was winter camp. We would leave the Friday after Thanksgiving for the rest of the weekend. At this camp, only our troop would use the camp. We slept in the mess hall and ate there also. There was a woodstove we could use for heat and cooking.

I volunteered to do all the cooking with other scouts helping if I needed them, and they would do all the dishes. I was limited in my cooking skills but felt I could do this. Dad went with me to buy the food for about twenty-five boys and went over each meal and how to make them. The year before, Dad actually went to winter camp with us and might have helped with some cooking. But this year he was not going. Evidently Dad still enjoyed scouting, and if he wasn't so busy with business, probably he would have been in scouting.

Just to make a long story shorter, I got through this weekend, two breakfasts, two lunches, and two dinners. I know one dinner was Dad's meatloaf recipe. And remember that all the cooking was done on an old woodstove. The big negative was I was tied to cooking all the time. Done with one meal, getting ready for the next while the others were out enjoying the time. But no regrets, it was a good experience, and the campers said it was good.

One last story on scouting. We hiked in the month of June for some twenty miles on the Appalachian Trail through mountainous terrain. It was a three- or four-day hike from Water Gap to Wind Gap near the Delaware River. It was one of the most interesting experience I ever had. There were only our scoutmaster and a college student helping, named Jack Smith, who had a long scouting history, and I believe was an Eagle scout with only about eight scouts.

We had our backpacks, tents, food, and change of clothes, but only one canteen of water each. We were depending on the springs marked on our map for more water. Guess what? We could only find one spring. The weather was extremely hot, and we were carrying a heavy load. We came across a Buddhist retreat building and found a water hand pump. We had chlorine tablets with us, and we all used them, just in case the water was bad.

On the last day of our hike, four young men camp upon us and said they would be getting off very soon, and each had extra water canteens. They gave four canteens to us with an address to send them when we finished.

The trail was marked by paint on trees and on shale rock because undergrowth would quickly cover any path not being used very often. We came across a very wide patch of shale, maybe one hundred yards, and the paint was washed off, and we were sure we were lost. Remember no cell phones! After looking in every direction, we found the painted trees again.

Mr. Druckenmiller, Drucky, met us at our destination,point which was a diner along a highway, about Sunday noon with another car to take us back but again, the person he was, took us to the diner and bought us our meal. Another great experience!

A special note, Scoutmaster Milligan came to know the Lord late in life watching the television broadcast of Faith Baptist Church and visited us there until he was physically unable.

14

Bad Boy, School Days

I don't think of myself as a bad child because we were taught to be kind, and Mom, especially, reminded us to love and take care of one another and show respect to adults and anyone over us, especially schoolteachers.

There were a few times I got in trouble and could have been in a lot more if I would have been caught, but, for the most part, it was clean fun with no intent to hurt anyone.

As a boy of about four years old, my friend Jack Bedford and I got into our next-door neighbor's garage, opened paint cans, and threw the paint all over the inside of the garage, windows, walls, garage door, and floor. When I went into my house, I was covered with paint and confessed what we did. The man's garage belonged to good friends Al and Betty Lawrence.

My dad, with Mr. Bedford, scraped the windows, and some-time later, the inside of the garage was repainted, probably by Dad and Mr. Bedford. I don't remember being spanked, but I was severely scolded.

When I was in the fourth grade, of course, we had to walk back and forth to school, which was a good walk of maybe a mile away, and we walked this four times a day. To keep us students safe, there were crossing safeties made up of older children sponsored by the Pottstown Triple A Club. These were children in the seventh and eighth grades who wore white belts around the waist and across the chest to identify these specially trained students.

One of the crossing guards was a sister to a friend of mine. At Main and Park Avenue where she crossed us, we with about four or five other students decided we would cross not where the guards were, but up the street away from the corner. We knew this was wrong, and we could be in trouble, but we figured she would not turn us in. She warned us two days in a row. The third day she told the school principal, a man named Lloyd Weisel, who could be very stern and someone you didn't want to get into trouble with.

He came to our fourth-grade room and called out our names written on a paper. As we came to the front of the class, he grabbed each one of us by the back of our necks and threw us out into the hall. We could hardly keep our balance, but the embarrassment in front of the whole class was punishment enough. He then lectured us in his loud, stern voice that the whole class could hear every word. Needless to say, we never had a problem crossing at the exact corner and obeying the safety guards.

The interesting rest of this story is that seventh and eighth grades were moved to Perkasie, and when I was in sixth grade, I was chosen by the new principal, Mrs. Case, to be captain of the crossing guards and rewarded with a two-day trip by bus to Washington DC, with the other area school district captains. It was a great experience and the first time I slept in a large hotel and saw the great capital city.

PS: I never told my parents about the scolding from Mr. Weisel and that brother Paul was also involved in this.

I mentioned about walking back and forth to school about four miles every day. This, in itself, was an experience because there were always so many things to see, talk about, and do. If we had any money, we would stop at Fritz's Drugstore next to the trolley station to buy penny candy and drive Fritz Schuleben crazy when we couldn't make up our minds which ones we wanted or change our minds on our selection.

If we heard a trolley coming, we would put a penny on the track and let the trolley smash it flat and oblong.

For fifteen cents, we could buy a milkshake at Kreb's Drugstore at Main and Temple in the Odd Fellows Hall with no ice cream and twenty cents with ice cream.

Before the incident with the crossing guards, we would hide behind the solid cement walls about four feet high on Main Street as you approach Church Street. They still stand there today. It was dangerous because we would hang on to the top of the wall with our fingers and our feet on only a three-inch ledge. If we fell, it was about two stories high, and we would have easily broken a leg. No one ever fell, and we were never reported.

Just enjoying the change in seasons and the stores decorated for each new holiday made each walk special. Of course, we would run or race and watch the 309 traffic that was fairly heavy all day. Life was never boring; there was always something to look forward to.

Sellersville elementary school where we got really smart.

Touching on my first six years in school, there was no kindergarten, so I started in first grade. It was the building on Church

Street, the lower right-hand room. The Sellersville Museum now occupies the premises.

The first day in school, Mrs. Clara Day, our good teacher, kept the former first graders in the room for maybe a half hour to create a friendly atmosphere for us new children. One of the things she had us do was form a circle around the room with the former students between each of us. She played music on her windup Victrola, and we marched around in a circle.

Charlie Myers, who later became a sports reporter for the local newspapers, suddenly turned around to me and said, "Do you know how to tie your shoes?"

I responded yes. I'll never know why he asked the question, but I never forgot.

I remember well learning to read the *Mac and Muff: Easy Growth in Reading*, learning to write numbers, especially the number 8. She taught this by having you take a train ride as you circled and crossed over the track to complete the number 8.

During our rest periods, she played the Victrola and always the same two songs. I love the songs because it really did make you want to put your head on your desk and close your eyes to rest. One was "Sweet and Low" and "The Donkey Serenade."

A sad note, Ms. Day lost her brother Edward in the war. He was a graduate of the US Naval Academy and a fighter pilot.

The school janitor was a kind older man named Mr. Eberly. Heated with coal and a school bell, he rung for recesses to come in. A school hygienist, Mrs. Frederick cleaned all the students' teeth twice a year.

I believed I was an average student, except in history. History was easy and exciting. I also enjoyed art and should have pursued some training in it.

In sixth grade, I won first prize in the American Legion Poppy Poster Contest.

I have memories from each grade and the teachers—Ms. Day, Mrs. Moyer, Ms. Neiman, Ms. Baum, Ms. Daub, and Ms. Bloomgardener who became Mrs. Case.

Ms. Daub taught fifth grade and lived at Green and Penn Streets, right behind the school. She also taught my father in school. Ms. Day went to school with my dad. Mrs. Bloomgardener was new to the school that year and was principal, and I enjoyed this class also. I seemed to have a good relationship with her and did well in this class also.

We always looked forward to recess time, which was played on an all dirt ground next to the school that could have ashes mixed in it from the coal furnace. Four maple trees that always looked half-dead were in a line about twenty-five feet from the school that always seemed to be in our way in order to play.

One of the favorite games we played was horse and rider champion. The bigger boy would be the horse, and a small but strong boy would straddle his hips and back. The horse, in a standing upright position, would attack another set of boys and try to throw them of the horse. Being the biggest kid, I was never defeated, no matter who was on my back. When I was in first grade, I weighed eighty-five pounds.

I believe I was in third or fourth grade, and we had to complete a page in a spelling or grammar book before we could go to recess. There was one question I could not complete for whatever reason, so I took my eraser and simply erased it out of the page. The paper was the soft paper often found in coloring books. I took the paper, laid it on the teacher's desk, and hurried out the door. The teacher never said a word. Later, she either laughed to herself or just gave me a great break.

Childhood diseases were big issues in our lives and at school. You would miss two to three weeks of school if you contracted measles or chickenpox. I had both of them. You would be quarantined at home for the entire length required.

The measles seemed to be treated the most serious. We often spread it to other family members. In some ways, that was good, so we would all miss school and be treated as a family.

The board of health, which was Police Chief Mike Hallman, with directions from your doctor, would post a large sign on your door stating the quarantine for whichever disease and future instructions. We could never leave the house.

The milkman, Harvey Clymer (no family relative), could leave the milk bottles but could not pick them up. He would leave crates because it could be three weeks of more of bottles. When the doctor cleared you of the disease, Mike Hallman would come back with a machine that sprayed an antiseptic in each room to supposedly kill the germs. Up and down stairs, he would spray; it was almost like a smoke bomb.

We passed our time doing homework, crayoning books, the radio, and playing table games, like checkers. The first time I ever sewed anything was during this time. Mother was home at the time, and we were bored, so she gave us a small piece of cloth, about two feet square, and said we should make something out of it. Cut it with scissors and sew it with needle and thread. I cut little pockets about two inches wide and four inches long with a rounded bottom and open top to put something in it—the beginning of my future journey or something.

During one of these illnesses, our sister, Anne (Anna to us), became our nurse. We had her running, it seemed all the time, for things to eat or toys we needed, since we were in our bedroom during the early and more critical time of the illness. Mother would remind us what a good sister we had and should stop teasing her when we got well. Here again, she began her nursing career, and she has a lot to thank us for; something good came out of all this sickness.

It is interesting how the medical world has changed since our childhood. It seemed like every other child was going to the hospital to get their tonsils removed. Today, nobody has this procedure done. Also, appendicitis was like an epidemic. Children and young people were having them removed constantly. You always prayed you weren't next.

I never remember the school being closed for these diseases, but at times, the rooms were pretty empty. The only time they were closed was around 1950 when several children developed polio. Now that was really scary because no one wanted to live in an iron lung machine.

They did close all the schools for a couple of weeks because it was unknown where this illnesses came from and how it was spread. Two of the boys were from the high school football team and thought it could be spread by contact.

After a few days, while living on Green Street around 1950, some neighbors and I decided to sneak onto the elementary school grounds to play. How dumb can you be? The head principal of the whole school system, Mr. Louis Snyder, lived on Green Street also, and his garage bordered on the school playground. You're right—he drove up the alley, and we were dead. He got out of his car and really gave us a scolding and sent us home.

Discipline within the Clymer house was easy because we were all such good children. Well, we weren't all that bad. We were typical for the time, I guess.

Our parents taught us right and wrong, especially our mother. She taught us basic Christian principles that she expected us to live by, especially respect for adult people. If we got in school trouble, expect double when you got home. So school trouble, if any, was never carried home, and we never complained about a teacher.

Mother was the enforcer. We very seldom got spanked, but Mother would hit us, shout at us because we really did need it at times. Brother Robert seemed to have the worst temper, and I was second, if things did not go my way. I remember trying to open a stuck storm door at the front porch. It just would not open, so—*pow*—I punched my fist through the glass and then opened it. I did get a few small cuts, but it could have been really bad.

I remember when I did something wrong in the house and ran out the door with Mother running right behind me, and both of us running down the alley, but she could not catch me. Remember, she was only about thirty-one or thirty-two years old and could really run yet. So she turned around and stood in our backyard with me standing in the short alley between the pants factory and the end row house where Aunt Martha lived.

She simply hollered, "You have to come home some time."

And how true it was. I don't remember being hit when I came home, but I didn't come home for maybe an hour. But Dad was home by then, and I really did get a good scolding.

Mother could grab a belt, flyswatter—anything that was near her at the time—and hit us with it. We were usually assigned to a chair and had to sit there until we were told to get up. It was tough.

Dad was not always there, but home enough to control everything. All he had to do was raise his voice, and usually that was enough. He never really hit us, not more than one swing with a hand across our backside, and we got the message. His favorite discipline was picking you up and throwing you into a padded living room chair and saying, "Don't move till I tell you."

The thing that is very important in all our disciplining was our parents loved us. We knew this, even though they were not huggy, kissy parents, but we knew by their actions and love coming to us from them. They would speak kindly to us, even though many times they were in a hurry, especially Mother. All the families I knew as a child were not the outward-affection type. The outward affection never started until many years later as I was in adult life.

I mentioned brother Bob had a bad temper as a little boy, and Mother, especially, was troubled how to handle him. Mother was the person who invented waterboarding. Only kidding. But she would put his head under the kitchen faucet with his head faced down to stop his screaming, and it always worked.

I also remember another time when Mother was spanking him with a short plastic hairbrush, and the brush broke in half with him lying across Mother's lap. Tough backside or weak brush!

Dad, in his business relationship, made friends in Perkasie with E. Hubbert and Son Baseball Factory president. Hubbert was considering getting into manufacturing a new style of glove called a trappers mitt or glove. It was made for first basemen position. It had a wide, solid leather webbing where you would catch the ball. Hubbert had the patterns, leather, and padding, but they needed someone to sew and lace the gloves. Dad was given the task to make about a half dozen or more for samples. The gloves looked great; I mean, really professional. They had a great feel and really worked well. I know because I got one. Dad gave me one because I usually played first base in our sandlot baseball. I was proud of it because everyone wanted to know about it, and then I could tell them my dad made it. At first, no one believed it. Even Drucky saw it.

Dad made another glove for Fred Christman, a state trooper living and working in the Quakertown Barracks who played softball in a league in Quakertown. I was there when Dad gave it to him. He was at the barracks at the time, and Fred was really taken aback by it.

The future of the glove probably ended up with Wilson Sporting Goods whom Hubbert made many of their balls for, and then were made offshore like most athletic products ended up. But it was great experience, and I think I had the glove playing for Faith Baptist Church in our softball league. I no longer have it.

While I'm talking about athletic gear, Ziggy Shelly, the plumber who was the general manager and much more to the Sellersville Greenjackets football team, would see us kids in the neighborhood and tell us to come to his plumbing garage at a set time, usually Saturday mornings. He would hand out the old, worn-out football equipment. Most were too big for us, but we took the old leather helmets, shoulder pads, football numbered shirts, and anything else that was free. It gave us a good feeling we had the same equipment the big guys had.

15

A Typical Week

A typical week in our home on Hughes Avenue—we will start with Sunday.

Sunday morning we would be getting ready for Sunday school at St. Michael's Lutheran Church. Dad would always drive us and drop us off. If it was a nice day, we would walk home, or Dad would tell us he was coming back for us, which was usually the case. We very seldom missed attendance there and would all strive to get our perfect attendance pins each year. One year I did not get a pin because I missed one or two weeks because of illness, and Dad was so mad at the church for not considering the illnesses.

I still remember many of the children's hymns and songs. I remember one song, in particular, that had a great melody but taught false Bible doctrines based on Lutheran beliefs.

The words went, "I was made Christian when my name was given, one of God's dear children and an heir of heaven."

What they are teaching is in your infant baptism, you became a Christian. This is a false teaching and ruins the heart of the Christian faith. Where is the faith in the finished work of Christ that must be believed to receive forgiveness of sins? Can an infant believe and repent?

I did gain basic Bible knowledge concerning Christ but little about the Bible doctrine and stories. I was religious and lost at this time.

There were some nice teachers in the system who were also public school teachers who were capable and interesting but were hindered by the liberal, modernistic material coming into the church. Most teaching was centered on our relationships with other people and living a moral life.

By the time we got home, we were hungry like all kids, but we had to change our Sunday dress clothing to play clothing. I had developed a bad pattern of changing my clothing and leaving them on a pile on the bedroom floor to get to lunch. Mother would pick them up for me but was after me to pick them up myself, which I never did. Finally she said she would not pick them up again, and I would wear them the next week exactly as I left them. The clothes lay there for about two days, and I know I could not wear my suit all wrinkled next Sunday, so my life changed forever. I began to pick up my clothes and hang them in the closet. From that day forth and as much as I remember, I have never left my clothes lying around. They always had a place or were put in the laundry.

Usually the noon meal was not ready yet when we came downstairs, so we looked forward to the Sunday comics. *Prince Valiant* was my favorite. It was a continuing story about a prince in the Middle Ages who rode a white horse and administered justice in those Dark Ages. Unlike most comics that consumed only a small portion of space on each page, he was given the whole page because each picture was a work of art. They probably could have been framed if they were not printed on newspaper.

Of course, I read *Dick Tracy, The Phantom, Dagwood Bumstead, Mark Trail, Li'l Abner, Mutt and Jeff,* and many more. Even more than today, this was a special treat every Sunday.

Our Sunday-noon meal became the biggest of the week. Dad almost always made it. We had roast beef or meatloaf, very seldom chicken or turkey. Mashed potatoes, two vegetables, milk, bread and butter, gravy and always a dessert, usually a store-bought cake.

In the afternoon, Dad would take a nap unless the Philadelphia Eagles were on the radio. The Eagles had some of their best teams in 1947, 1948, and 1949. They were coached by Greasy Neal; Steve

VanBuren, Bosh Pritchard, Ben Kish, the running backs; Tommy Thompson at quarterback, Al Wistert, their star tackle; Jack Hinkle at end; Peter Pihois at the other end; Joe Jakowitz at center, and Vick Sears, tackle.

There was a time not too long ago I could name every position player because they went both ways on offense and defense. We would be glued to the radio as By Saam would give you the game as the announcer.

I later met and got Al Wistert's autograph when he was the banquet speaker for the Greenjackets championship years in 1949 and 1950. Dick Coll and I were the water boys for those years.

On other Sunday afternoons, we read our comics, listened to the radio, including listening to the Phillies, which were really lousy until about 1949 and 1950 when the *Whiz Kids* came on the scene.

Sellersville bakery, later Yeakels Bakery, still looks like it did when I was a boy.

Sunday supper or dinner was a trip to the Sellersville bakery on Walnut Street, which later became Yeakel's Bakery. Dad would buy about two-dozen glazed doughnuts. These were the soggy kind and fresh made that day and a pint box of Hershey ice cream that he would cut in half with a butcher's knife to give each of us one-half the box in a bowl with two doughnuts each, and that was our Sunday supper.

When you went to the bakery on Sunday afternoon, you had to stand in line from the pavement up about eight to ten wooden steps, across the porch and into the store itself. It must have been worth the wait because it was Sunday after Sunday.

While eating this meal, it was time to listen on the radio to the *Shadow*, starring Lamont Cranston and Margo Lanes. He had the ability to disappear at least in our minds and reappear to startle and capture the evil people of that time. Where are you now? We could use a hero like you. He spoke in a normal, kind voice, except when closing in on the baddies he would use his eerie voice and remind all that the "Shadow knows" and then laugh.

Following the *Shadow* were radio family-type shows such as *Henry Aldridge* or *Fibber McGee and Molly*, and *The Jack Benny Program* with Dennis Day and Rochester. These shows were great because of the voices behind the microphones and audience use of our imaginations.

It was a wonderful time in those evenings as your parents usually sat and listened and laughed at the shows, while we children played on the carpeted floors with the large metal grate bringing warmth from the coal heater in the basement. Sunday was really a family day for us. By 9:00 PM, it was time for bed and to begin a new week tomorrow.

Just a postscript: we had a rat in the basement under the wood-pile, used for starting a fire or in the coal bin. Dad got another neighbor to help with the kill. George Huff came in to help. We had to stay upstairs with the cellar door closed so the rat could not escape. I think they killed it, but I'm not sure how. They had shovels and other tools in hand to do the job, so they must have killed it because we were allowed back into the cellar afterward. But it was exciting for the moment.

Mondays through Fridays, all seemed to run together, except for the different radio programs in the evening that helped distinguish the days. If it was a school day, we were up early, dressed, and eating our cereals. It was usually because our radio programs that were designed for us kids to use their box tops in order to send for the super gadgets and rings, decoders, etc., to keep America safe and us happy.

Kellogg's Corn Pops, Wheaties, Kix, Cheerios, Corn Flakes, Shredded Ralston, etc., were all cereals available to us. There were always a sticky bun, ice bun, potato bun, shoofly, and funny cakes at breakfast available and usually one or two at a breakfast.

We would be usually back up the steps and brushing our teeth. There was one day Paul came running down the steps screaming his mouth was on fire and that it was burning. Mother washed his mouth with water and found out he used Bengay ointment from a tube, which is used for sore muscles and joints and creates heat. His teeth could have fallen out.

Left to Right: Brother Dave, myself, Robert. In our back yard.

At noon, we would walk home from school, which was about a mile away. Mother would come home from the pants factory and make eggs or sandwiches, like peanut butter and jelly, or lunchmeat and more breakfast buns before it was time to go back.

We usually knew what our supper was going to be because Mother usually went with a weekly set of meals with some variations. She usually got the food ready and gave instructions to the sitter what she wanted done and when to start the meal. We had meat, such as beef or pork at every supper, and potatoes with a vegetable, a dessert, and always milk at every meal. We had a strange custom as I look back now, but anytime we wanted more milk, we would rock the bottom of our glasses on the table to tell Mother we wanted more milk. She would refill our glass by using the quart bottles left on the table because we always needed refills.

Because there was such a difference in Paul's size and myself, there was a period of time Paul would be given the cream from the top of the bottle being the milk was not homogenized. She thought this would help him.

When we came home from school, we would change our school clothes into our play clothes and to the bread box for Tastykakes or jelly roll, whatever was there for us. Then out into the street to play our games or sports. Then four thirty would come, and it was back into our homes to listen to our favorite radio programs. Then supper and everyone would be there. There was never a time when anyone was missing for any reason. Not even Dad was missing, as busy as he was. If he went back to work, it was always after supper.

Life was busy, but not hectic with demands put on family today to be everywhere, but where they should be. Even when I served papers, I ate with family before I left.

We were encouraged to do our homework. We never seemed to have a lot of it, or maybe we didn't do too much of it.

If we had Cub Scouts or Boy Scouts, this would take us out of the house at night. Otherwise, we looked forward to the radio programs, especially the Lone Ranger, which came on Wednesday night with Tonto and the William Tell Overture music to thrill us as we were glued to the radio.

Suppertime was a talking time about the day, future plans, and general news of the things happening in town or our relatives, so we sort of got a feeling for everything concerning politics, the president, the war, people at work, work ethics, morality, etc. It wasn't always direct teaching but inferences on subject matter.

I knew Dad was a Republican at an early age and would not vote for Roosevelt, but he thought he was the right man for the Depression to get people and the country moving. He made friends in town easily with Republicans, though he had friendships with everyone. He ran for town council and received the highest amount of votes of anyone. He continued in the council until he built his new home in West Rockhill in 1963.

By nine or nine thirty, we were up in bed, and I remember saying my simple Now I Lay Me Down to Sleep prayer I said every night that Mother taught us when we were still very young. Once in a great while, Dad would tell us a story like *Jack and the Beanstalk*.

My favorite story Mother would tell us was the little match girl. She could tell this with all the emotion and how sorry you felt as the poor little girl used up all her matches to stay warm and died at the end of the story.

As an adult I often felt this was actually my mother, but she lived at the end and had her family. But she was the poor little struggling girl who grew up poor in Philadelphia.

Saturday was no school day, so it was a good day. When I look back now at my life on Hughes Avenue, we did very little work around the house. Mother just wanted us out of her way so she could get the work done and only wanted us to stay out of trouble. Just like the other kids on the street, we were free to play. We would be out playing in the morning or inside on rainy days—coloring books and reading comic magazines, books, etc. If it snowed, we would be sledding in the street and hated to see Phil Coll come with the cinder truck in the borough to cinder the street. They had two men on the back of the truck, hand shoveling the cinders onto the street after it was plowed.

Even though we did not have to work in our homes, we were not lazy. I mentioned babysitting David in the child sulky or stroller, having a paper delivery job, and then shoveling snow for people, especially if school was cancelled. We never gave a price; it was whatever they wanted to give us—fifty cents or less was okay because you could buy a candy bar for five cents in those days.

Lunch on Saturday was always spaghetti with the meat cooked with the spaghetti sauce and noodles, and we had Mother's good coleslaw. More play in the afternoon or Dad would take us and Mother to the Plaza Movie Theater in Perkasie for an afternoon show. As

I mentioned earlier, Tuesday nights was another time for the double-feature country cowboy movies.

Saturday-night supper was exciting because we could make our own fried hamburger from ground beef into patties and fry them on our gas kitchen stove. Usually we didn't have rolls, so we ate them between two pieces of bread with ketchup and sometimes onions.

Friends would sometimes visit on a Saturday night or Sunday afternoon, but there was not an excess of this, and when friends called, we as children would be quiet and listen to the adults. Aunt Martha and Uncle Frank were relatives who came regularly because they lived close and had no other family. Uncle Irvin and Aunt Amelia lived either in Allentown or Philadelphia during the war, and then they moved back to Perkasie before retiring to the Pocono Mountains.

Left to Right: Dad's sister Aunt Martha and
Uncle Frank with Mom and Dad.

When we visited Aunt Martha and Grammy Clymer, we would be served ginger ale and pretzels every time, which was fine with us.

The other food given us—and I would always look for as a little boy—was a special candy glass with a dome on the top filled with chocolate nonpareils, the small coin-shaped chocolates with white sugar tiny pearls coating the tops. I have that glass in my home today and treasure it immensely for the memories.

The QuakerTown Farmers Market and auction, now known as the Q-Mart, was another important aspect of our family's life while living on Hughes Avenue, as well as afterward.

I can never remember a Saturday that we were not at what we always called the auction. Besides our grocery store shopping and bakers, hucksters, milkmen serving our home, our dad would always go to the auction. He would always buy a bushel basket of potatoes usually from Auckland's Potato Farm. Never knowing that later in my life, my daughter would marry into this family, and John Auckland's son, David, would be a major spiritual influence and my pastor for many years.

Our father's brother Uncle Irvin and Aunt Amelia at their 50th wedding anniversary.

Dad would also buy bushel baskets of apples from produce growers, as well as other fruits and vegetables. Just to walk through was exciting; it was always packed with people and so much to see and eat, although we very seldom ate there. They were well-known for the fried-fish sandwiches. They fried the fresh fish in front of you and sandwiched it between two pieces of white bread. You put on your own condiments. Another stand had home-made potato chips, cooked right there also. You couldn't get it any fresher.

There were clothing stands; shoes, jewelry, and meats were always very big there. Dad would often buy meats there also.

A few things of interest were the whole floor was a dirt floor, but there was very little dust from all of the traffic because they kept it oiled with, I believe, motor oil. It had a dark, very-smooth finish that almost looked like linoleum. When you purchased your fruit and vegetables from at least a dozen hucksters, you could not pick your own. You had to stand at the front of the stand, blocked by counter tables, and point to the attendees who picked them for you. If you got a bad orange or other fruit, the next week people would let them know. You would have stands that sold watermelon, which, in the summer, would be sold outside with another dozen stands that sold produce and have them plug a melon. They would cut a two-inch square with their large blade knife and pull out some melon for you to taste. You always bought it.

One of the most exciting things my parents ever bought me was at the auction. Every week I would look at a store that sold work shoes, cowboy boots, and fireman-type rubber boots. Well, I saw these rubber boots that were a cross between a Western and fireman's boot. They were dark brown that come up below my knee. You had to remove your shoes to wear them and had to be slid on since there was no front opening. I had to have them, and every week, I would continue to ask for them. Can you imagine this, me, such a pain to continue to ask and then it happened! I got my boots, and I did enjoy them till, like everything, I outgrew them.

The first thing I headed for the next day was the small stream of water coming through the field where we built our forts and foxholes to test them.

The Lord was so good to me and our family as I was growing up. He protected and directed our lives as we were blessed beyond anything I can put into my mere writings. I will never understand it all but I see now how He moved and brought us all to His wonderful salvation provided in Jesus Christ.

Well, how much more can I write about? A lot is still in my head, and that's where it will stay, I guess for a little while yet. I hope whoever reads this will enjoy it just a little bit. I had the privilege to see it and actually live it, and it was a joy to write it and send me back again to this grandest of time in my life.

Dad sold the house in 1948 to the Kline family from Perkasie, as we were now moving to 27 Green Street in Sellersville in a house that Dad said he always admired, even from his youth. It was built and owned by Jim Cressman, who had connections with the Philadelphia Athletics Baseball Team and would bring players for picnics at the house. It was even pictured on postcards around 1909-1914, and I have some of these pictures today.

Pictures of our Green Street home from a post card
about 1920. We moved there in 1948.

When Kline asked for the keys to the house, Dad said he never had any all the time we lived there, even on vacations. That was on Hughes Avenue. That was my time, the Greatest Generation.

That's all, folks.

The End

After we all grew up. Left to Right: My brothers and sister, Barry, Gerald, David, Frank, Anna, Robert, Paul.

One More Thought

This book covers only twelve years of my life, such a short time. I have often thought how long eternity is, and I'm sure you have too and where will we be during that time.

One question, have you ever been wrong in your life, especially when you thought you were absolutely, positively correct? You cannot be wrong about eternity. Please don't let pride keep you from God's way. Jesus said He is the only way. How can you be sure of this?

A few proven facts to know and believe:

- He met and fulfilled innumerable prophesies made thousands years before He was born. The odds of this happening is one chance in 13 trillion that only Jesus could match these prophecies of the Messiah.
- His miracles and His life are more proof.
- He said and proved He was God from all eternity.
- He came for the main purpose to die for our sins and did it exactly as the prophesies said He would.
- His blood would be shed on a cross to pay for our sins. This was God's plan of love for us.
- He would arise from the dead. This was testified to by over five hundred people over forty days. This was the ultimate evidence of His Deity.
- There are many more proofs why we can put our faith in Jesus Christ and trust Him for our eternity.

If you know you are a sinner and tell the Lord you are, ask the Lord to forgive you and believe that Christ loved you and died for your sins. Simply tell the Lord you want to receive Christ as your own Savior and to change your life to His.

God, who cannot lie, will do this as it is plainly stated in His word, the Bible. God said He will give you eternal life. He wants you to know this, that you have become His child for now and all eternity. Please find a good Bible-teaching church that will help you in your new life.

The Lord's plan is to give us eternal life by trusting in Christ alone, not in a church or by working our way as all other world religions teach.

Your biggest mistake will be making no decision. May the Lord give you insight, understanding, and courage to make this decision. You will never ever be sorry you did.

> That if you confess with your mouth Jesus is Lord, and believe in your heart that God raised him from the dead, you will be saved. For it is with your heart that you believe and are justified, and it is with your mouth that you confess and are saved. As the Scripture says, Anyone who trusts in him will never be put to shame. For there is no difference between Jew and Gentile—the same Lord is Lord of all and richly blesses all who call on him, for, Everyone who calls on the name of the Lord will be saved. (Romans 10:9-13, New International Version)